# Excel 2024
# Useful Functions

## EXCEL 2024 ESSENTIALS - BOOK 3

### M.L. HUMPHREY

# SELECT TITLES BY M.L. HUMPHREY

## EXCEL 2024 ESSENTIALS
Excel 2024 for Beginners
Intermediate Excel 2024
Excel 2024 Useful Functions

## EXCEL 365 ESSENTIALS
Excel 365 for Beginners
Intermediate Excel 365
102 Useful Excel 365 Functions

## EXCEL ESSENTIALS 2019
Excel 2019 Beginner
Excel 2019 Intermediate
Excel 2019 Formulas & Functions

## EXCEL ESSENTIALS
Excel for Beginners
Intermediate Excel
50 Useful Excel Functions
50 More Excel Functions

## WORD ESSENTIALS
Word for Beginners
Intermediate Word

## POWERPOINT ESSENTIALS
PowerPoint for Beginners
Intermediate PowerPoint

## ACCESS ESSENTIALS
Access for Beginners
Intermediate Access

See mlhumphrey.com for all titles by M.L. Humphrey

# CONTENTS

# CONTENTS (CONT.)

# Introduction

If you truly want to use Excel to its utmost, you have to learn how to use formulas and functions. Even if you're going to use it for text-based uses (which I do sometimes), there are functions that let you clean up text that are very useful to know, in addition to the many, many, many functions that perform actual mathematical calculations.

Now, this is the fourth time I've written a series of books on Microsoft Excel. And because I am wired weird, I like to actually write these books from scratch each time. I know what I've done before and sometimes reuse portions, but each time I sort of step back and say, "What should I cover in this book?" And even, "How many books should this series include?"

Functions is one of those areas where I've gone back and forth the most. The first time around, I started with just two books, *Excel for Beginners* and *Intermediate Excel*. I only covered a handful of functions in those books: SUM, IF, COUNTIFS, SUMIFS, CONCATENATE, and a special use of the TEXT function. I figured your average beginner really didn't need much more. And if they did, they could use Help to find it.

I wrote that entire series of books with the singular goal of teaching self-published authors how to use pivot tables, so I was trying to get to that point as fast as possible. Later, though, I ended up writing two more books in that series, *50 Useful Excel Functions* and *50 More Excel Functions*, that covered a hundred functions between them, with a chapter devoted to each one.

That was a lot, and it put me right at the edge of my comfort level to cover that many in detail, because I don't use that many day-to-day. But I wanted a good selection of functions across various uses for the variety of potential users who might read those books.

Some of the chapters were also very short. I included certain functions for completeness' sake. For example, I don't think I have ever used the PRODUCT function (which multiplies values), but I included it because I wanted to explain SUMPRODUCT (which sums the results of multiplied values across more than one range).

So the next time around I covered functions in only one book, which I think worked, too. But that book was bordering on being a little too much for someone to read cover-to-cover.

(And, yes, I really do hope that people will read this book that way, even though it's the length of a short novel.)

I did the same thing with the Excel 365 books.

Which leads us to now. There is so much that Excel can do, it can be overwhelming. I think I add value by cutting out the extraneous mess you don't need. I don't want to write a dictionary of Excel, others have done that, and probably more effectively. My thought is, "You have limited time, I have limited time, let's focus on what you might actually use some day."

But there still are times when it makes sense to cover a lesser-used function so you know it exists. Or to at least mention a different function so you'll recognize it if someone else uses it.

There are also a lot of good new Excel functions that even experienced users should learn to use like XLOOKUP, TEXTBEFORE, TEXTAFTER, TEXTJOIN, RANDARRAY, and IFS. But some of the core functions still do great work. The SUM or count functions are probably the functions you will use the most in Excel, no matter how sophisticated you get.

So as I wrote this book, I asked myself over and over, "Does this user need to know this right now?" Which led me to cover 50 functions in their own chapter and reference another 20, so 70 in total. I think that's a good solid base for you to start from.

If you must skip around, and I know some of you will, I've given you a chapter that lists the top functions I think you should learn, so at least cover those. You don't have to use them, but read those chapters to understand what's possible in Excel.

Also, be sure to read the non-function-specific chapters at the beginning and end of the book, because they apply no matter what functions you use.

Finally, I print these books in black and white to make them as affordable for readers as possible, but sometimes it is nice to see color images. The ebook versions of these books are in color and if you go to the About the Author section at the end of this book there is a discount code for buying the ebook off of my Payhip store.

Okay, then. First things first, we need to learn the basics of what formulas and functions are, where to find them, and how to use them.

# Formulas Versus Functions

You can have a formula in Excel that does not include a function. But you cannot have a function in Excel without it being part of a formula.

Every formula in Excel is started with an equals sign ( = ), a minus sign ( - ), or a plus sign ( + ). That tells Excel, "This·is a calculation or task that needs to be performed. It's not just text or a numeric value to store, I want you, Excel, to do something for me."

I personally start all of my formulas with the equals sign, but some people will come from a background where using the minus or plus sign works better for them. No matter which one you use, Excel will convert it to a formula that uses an equals sign.

Here is an example of the same calculation written three different ways:

| What I Wrote | What Excel Changed It To | Visible Result |
|---|---|---|
| =4-2 | =4-2 | 2 |
| +4-2 | =4-2 | 2 |
| -2+4 | =-2+4 | 2 |

The top row is how I would write it. This is basically saying, "Hey, Excel, take the number 4 and subtract the number 2":

$$=4\text{-}2$$

The second row starts the formula with a plus sign, but says the same thing:

$$+4\text{-}2$$

Excel changed that to:

$$=4\text{-}2$$

The third row starts the formula with a minus sign:

$$-2+4$$

Note I had to switch up the order of the numbers there to make it work. That's basically saying, "I have negative 2 here, can you add four to it?" Excel changed that to:

$$=-2+4$$

All three of the above formulas work to perform the same calculation. Personally, I find it easier to write =4-2, but you do you, whichever one works.

As you saw with the above examples, a formula can just include numbers and operator signs like minus ( - ) and plus ( + ) in one cell, which we'll cover in more detail in another chapter. But what makes Excel really powerful are two more things it can do: cell notation and functions.

Cell notation lets you shortcut the tedious task of typing in a bunch of numbers. While it is possible to write something like:

$$=1+2+3+4+5+6+7+8+9+10$$

or

$$=A1+A2+A3+A4+A5+A6+A7+A8+A9+A10$$

if those values are in cells in your worksheet, you can also just tell Excel to add a range of cells by using what I refer to as cell notation. A1:A10 refers to the values in Cells A1 through A10, for example. (We'll go into detail on that in a moment, too.)

Functions are basically a shorthand way to tell Excel what to do. For example, instead of the formula above where I put a plus sign between every single value I wanted to add, I can instead use the SUM function and cell notation:

$$=SUM(A1:A10)$$

tells Excel to go to the specified cells (A1 through A10), pull each value, and then add them all together.

SUM is one of the most basic functions in Excel, but there are far more complex functions that you can use. SUMIFS, for example, will take a range of values, compare them to your specified criteria, and only add the values where all of the criteria are met. I can tell Excel with one little function that I want it to add the dollar value of sales of blue widgets made to Colorado customers since July 1, 2024.

Giving Excel a function to use is like giving it an instruction sheet to follow. As long as you use the correct function, format your inputs correctly, and give the required inputs, Excel will do all the rest. That's the key, of course: Excel is only as good as the person using it. You give it bad commands or bad data, you will get bad results.

To summarize: A formula is essentially you telling Excel you need it to do something. You can have one formula per cell. A function is part of a formula. It's a shortcut way of telling Excel what you want it to do. A formula can include more than one function.

# Cell Notation

As I noted in the last chapter, cell notation is crucial to working with formulas and functions in Excel. If you don't know cell notation, you will not get near the full value from Excel that you could.

First, the basics.

A cell is referenced (by default) using its column letter and its row number. The first cell in any worksheet is Cell A1. The last cell in a worksheet in Excel 2024 is XFD1048576.

You should be able to see the column and row for a given cell without much issue, but if you ever have doubts, look to the left of the formula bar above the active workspace. That will show the cell reference for the cell you're in.

Here, for example, I am zoomed way out so that my column and row values are barely visible, but the formula bar stays the same size, and I can easily see that I'm in Cell AA28. (That only works, though, for a single cell. If you select a range of cells, that box will only show you the first selected cell in the range.)

To reference more than one cell, you have two options. You can use a comma ( , ) which you can think of as standing for *and*, or a colon ( : ) which you can think of as standing for *through*.

So if I write:

=SUM(A1,A2,A3)

that is saying to sum the values in Cells A1 *and* A2 *and* A3.

But I could also write that as:

$$=SUM(A1:A3)$$

which would be saying to sum the values in Cell A1 *through* Cell A3.

To reference an entire row or column, you just use the column letter or row number. So

$$=SUM(A:A)$$

will sum all values in Column A.

To sum across multiple columns or rows, start with the first letter or number, then use a colon, and end with the last letter or number in the range you want.

You can also combine commas and colons when referencing cells. So:

$$=SUM(6:8,11:12)$$

will sum the values in all cells in Rows 6 *through* 8 *and* in Rows 11 *through* 12.

If you want to reference cells in another worksheet or workbook, that is also possible.

For another worksheet in that workbook, write the name of the tab that has the data you want, followed by an exclamation point, and then the cell range. So:

$$=SUM(Operators!E10:E12)$$

is summing the values in Cells E10 through E12 in the worksheet named Operators in the current workbook.

To sum a worksheet in a different workbook, you can write the other workbook name in brackets, followed by the worksheet name in that workbook, followed by an exclamation point, followed by which cells to use:

$$=SUM([Book2]Sheet1!\$A\$1:\$E\$12)$$

If you're not sure how to reference a range of cells in a function, start it:

$$=SUM($$

and then when you reach the point in the function where you need the cell reference, select the cells you want by clicking and dragging. Excel will populate your function for you with the proper notation for those selected cells.

For cells I reference in other worksheets or other workbooks, I always do it that way because I can't be bothered to figure out how to write the worksheet or workbook reference portion properly.

You may still need to make edits, though.

I did that above for the last example, and Excel inserted $ signs for the cell range. Instead of writing A1:E12, it wrote $A$1:$E$12.

Using dollar signs has the effect of fixing that part of the cell reference. In this case, since it was on all parts of the cell range, that means that anywhere I copy that equation it will stay the same. Left as-is, the formula would continue to reference Cells A1 through E12 no matter where it was copied to. If I didn't want that, I'd have to remove them.

Those dollar signs have their uses. In the intermediate book, we were able to quickly build a two-variable analysis grid by fixing the row reference for the values across the top of the table and the column reference for the values down the side of the table.

So if you ever want to be able to copy a formula but keep one or more cell references in that formula fixed, use them.

This is probably a good time for a quick refresher on what happens to formulas when you copy them in Excel or cut them in Excel.

If you click on a cell that has a formula in it, *cut* that formula, and move it elsewhere, it will not change. Same with if you click on a cell, go to the formula bar, select the text from the formula bar, copy it, use Esc, go to another cell, and paste the text in.

If you *copy* a cell with a formula and paste it elsewhere, thought, the cell references in the formula will all update based on their new relative position.

This sounds horrible when you first hear about it, but that ability to copy a formula and have it adjust, is one of the most important things that Excel does for you.

Because let's say I have 100,000 rows of values in Column A and Column B, and for each row I want to add those values together. So I want =A1+B1 in Row 1, and then =A2+B2 in Row 2, and then =A3+B3 in Row 3, and so on for 100,000 rows.

I do not want to have to write 100,000 formulas to make that happen. And thanks to the beauty of how copied formulas work in Excel, I don't have to. All I have to do is write that first formula, =A1+B1, and then copy and paste it down 99,999 rows. Excel does all the rest for me.

But pay attention to this! Because copying and pasting formulas without fixing a cell reference is probably one of the most common mistakes I make.

For example, I will want to calculate the percentage share of each value in a table. That requires summing the total of all the values, and then dividing each individual value by the total. Here, for example, I have five values in Column A. The total of those values is 15:

| | A | B | C | D | E |
|---|---|---|---|---|---|
| 1 | Value | Bad Formula | Bad Result | Good Formula | Good Result |
| 2 | 1 | =A2/SUM(A2:A6) | 7% | =A2/SUM($A$2:$A$6) | 7% |
| 3 | 2 | =A3/SUM(A3:A7) | 14% | =A3/SUM($A$2:$A$6) | 14% |
| 4 | 3 | =A4/SUM(A4:A8) | 25% | =A4/SUM($A$2:$A$6) | 25% |
| 5 | 4 | =A5/SUM(A5:A9) | 44% | =A5/SUM($A$2:$A$6) | 44% |
| 6 | 5 | =A6/SUM(A6:A10) | 100% | =A6/SUM($A$2:$A$6) | 100% |
| 7 | | | | | |
| 8 | | | 190% | | 190% |
| 9 | | | | | |

In both Cells C2 and E2 I have correctly calculated the share of the value in Cell A2. You can see the formulas I used in Columns B and D:

$$=A2/SUM(A2{:}A6)$$

and

$$=A2/SUM(\$A\$2{:}\$A\$6)$$

Both give me 1 divided by 15, which is 7%.

Where the issue comes in is if I then copy that formula down to the rest of the cells in each column. For the formula used in Cell C2 (which you can see written out in Cell B2), when I copy it down, the formula adjusts *all* of the cell references.

By the time we reach Row 6, the formula in Cell C6 (shown in Cell B6) is:

$$=A6/SUM(A6{:}A10)$$

That is wrong. We are no longer dividing by the total of all five values. We know it's wrong because the value in Cell C6 is 100%, and the total of all values in Column C, shown in Cell C8, is 190%.

For the formula used in Cell E2 on the other hand, which you can see written out in Cell D2, when I copy it down, the formula only adjusts the top value because those dollar signs in the formula keep the other cell references fixed.

$$=A6/SUM(\$A\$2{:}\$A\$6)$$

Perfect. That's what we wanted.

It continued to reference the sum of the correct cell range, A2 through A6, that we wanted to divide by, while also updating the value that needed to be divided for each line.

(And for the extra credit students, if I'd just used A$2:A$6 that would've worked, too, since I'm staying in the same column, but I prefer to lock in the whole cell reference because that's actually what I'm trying to do.)

This is why you have to, have to, have to, gut check your results when working with formulas.

Or find another way to verify a result. Here in Cells C8 and E8 I've totaled my percentages, because I know that I need a total of 100% if I'm calculating a share of the whole. They don't total to 100% in Column C, so I know I made a mistake there.

Always ask yourself, "Does this result make sense?"

Excel is not smarter than you. Excel is as smart as you. It is you using a tool that is more sophisticated than a calculator, but at the end of the day, it's still you using a tool.

Okay. Now let's discuss functions more.

# Excel Function Basics

First, know that I will write all functions I refer to in this book with all caps, but you don't have to type them into Excel that way. So I'm going to write:

$$=SUM(A1:A10)$$

but you could type in

$$=sum(a1:a10)$$

and it would work just fine.

When you use a function, it needs to be followed by opening and closing parens.

Most functions will have required inputs that need to go between those parens—for example, SUM needs you to tell it what numbers to add together—but there are functions out there that do not require an input. For example TODAY() returns today's date.

You can use a function at any point in a formula.

$$=10-SUM(A1:A10)$$

is a perfectly valid formula that tells Excel to subtract the values in Cells A1 through A10 from 10.

Note that you don't put an equals sign before a function if it's not at the start of the formula. You just list it like you would any number in that formula.

You can also have more than one function in a single formula:

$$=SUM(A1:A10)+SUM(B1:B5)$$

is a perfectly valid formula that adds the values in Cells A1 through A10 and in Cells B1 through B5.

You can also "nest" functions. You do this when you put one function around another. For example:

$$=ROUND(SUM(A1:A10),2)$$

would sum the values in Cells A1 through A10, and then round the result to two decimal places.

If you nest functions, pay special attention to your opening and closing parens.

Sometimes it helps to think of a nested function as two parts:

$$=ROUND(x,2)$$

$$SUM(A1:A10)$$

where the x in the first function represents the second function. When you break two nested functions out this way, they should each stand on their own. ROUND would require a number there for x, but it is fully functional otherwise, with all required inputs and parens. SUM needs to be part of a formula, but it too is fully functional with all required inputs and parens.

# Excel Function Notation

For every function, Excel provides a text description of what the function does:

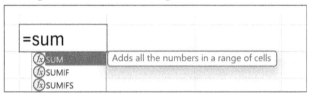

as well as a list of the inputs for that function:

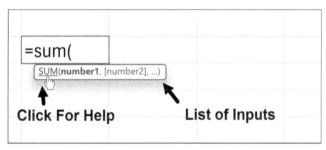

You can see above that the list of inputs for the SUM function are (number1, [number2], …)

Any input that's in plain text, like number1, is required. Any input in brackets, like number2, is optional. The dot, dot, dot at the end of a list means you can add more of the same inputs if needed.

So for SUM, that basically says, "The SUM function requires at least one number, but can take more than one. Separate each number you provide with a comma."

In this case, a "number" is very loosely defined, since it can be an actual number, a cell reference, a range of cells, or a named range.

$$=SUM(A1:B25)$$

is a perfectly legitimate use of SUM that only has one "number" input.

Other functions in Excel will have other types of inputs like TRUE/FALSE or lists where the value you provide specifies how that function works. (We will talk about them in detail under each specific function.)

When a function has multiple inputs that require different types of information, like XLOOKUP, you have to provide the inputs in the correct order with each input separated by a comma.

(It is possible to provide a list of values for an input into a function using curly brackets or a nested function. We'll cover a couple examples later, so don't worry about understanding how to do that right now.)

As you work through creating a function, the portion that is bolded in the description at any given time is the input you are currently being asked to give to Excel.

# Where To Find Functions & How to Use Them

I am going to spend the majority of this book walking you through some of the most useful functions I know in Excel. But chances are you are either going to forget a function name or you're going to need a different function. So before we dive in, I want to discuss where you can go to see *all* the available functions, and to search for one you want.

Excel has an entire tab devoted to Formulas. Click there on the Formulas tab, and you'll see a Function Library section with various categories (Recently Used, Financial, Logical, Text, Date & Time, Lookup & Reference, Math & Trig, and More).

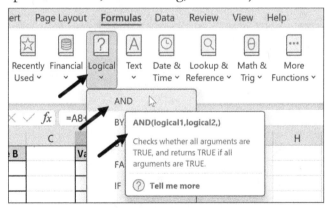

Each of those categories has a dropdown menu that alphabetically lists functions, like the one above for Logical. Hold your cursor over a function name to see a definition of what that function covers, like I have here for AND.

Personally, I don't think this is the ideal place to find a function you don't already know about, but it can be an interesting way to explore within a given category, like Text.

If you have a specific task in mind, it is better to bring up the Insert Function dialogue box. You can do this with Shift + F3, or, if like me you will never remember that, go to the Formulas tab and click on the Insert Function option on the far left:

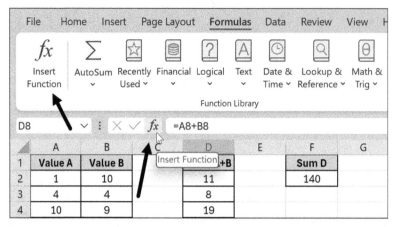

Another option is to click on the little function symbol in the formula bar that you can see above. However you do it, all three options will open the Insert Function dialogue box:

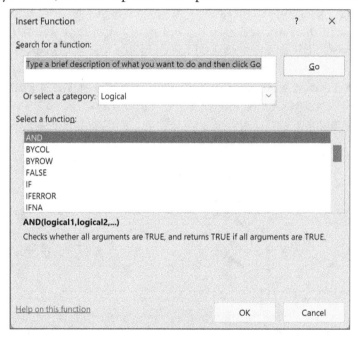

The Select a Category dropdown lets you choose a category and then see all functions for that specific category in the white box in the middle. But that's pretty much what you could do in the Formulas tab.

I prefer to search. Use the white Search For a Function field in the top section of the dialogue box to type a few keywords that describe what you're trying to do.

Click on Go and Excel will show you a list of possible functions in the Select A Function field in the middle of the dialogue box.

Click on each function in that list to see the function description and required inputs. Here I've searched for functions that let you "join text", andExcel gave me three options, CONCAT, CONCATENATE, and TEXTJOIN:

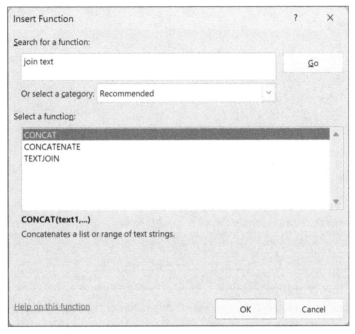

For each of the functions we're going to cover in detail in this book, I will give you that text description and list of inputs.

A few more things to point out here.

The Help On This Function link in the bottom left corner will bring up a web page that has help text specific to the selected function from the Microsoft website. (But only if you have your settings set to allow that.)

If you click OK, Excel is going to try to insert the selected function into the cell you were clicked into before you brought up the dialogue box.

It is also going to try to help you fill out the function with a Function Arguments dialogue box that will have fields for all of the required or optional inputs for that function.

On the next page is the one for TEXTJOIN, for example:

You can use this dialogue box if you find it helpful. It will show the result of the choices you've made in the bottom left corner where it says Formula Result =, which can be useful for a function you haven't used before.

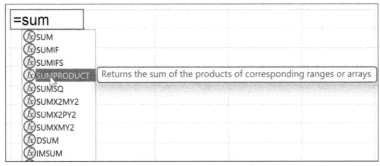

I personally prefer to work from the cell itself once I know what function I need, so let me walk you through how to do that now.

To start, go to the cell where you want your formula, and start entering it. When you reach the portion of your formula that requires a function, as you type the function name Excel will come up with a list that matches what you've typed so far:

You can click on any entry in that list to see what the function does without changing what you've already typed in the cell.

To use a function from that list, double-click on the function name. Excel will add it along with the opening paren.

I usually just type in the function name myself, so have to add that starting paren when I do so.

Once you have the function name and opening paren, the text below your cell will show the function name and its required inputs:

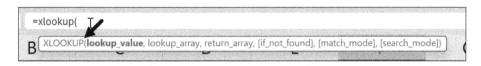

You can click on that function name to open the Help specific to that function.

A task pane should appear on the right-hand side of your workspace that is specific to that function.

(Note that this will only work if your options are set to allow help to open, otherwise you'll get an error message. Also, I can't promise that all Excel functions have their own dedicated help page, but the main ones do.)

If you click into the formula bar, you'll see the same text that you can link to help with and also the same list of inputs.

Either in the cell itself or in the formula bar, you then just walk through the function and provide each input as required. If this isn't a nested function, then close out the function with a closing paren when you reach the end.

* * *

One final tip for finding a function or figuring out how to use it: do a web search.

I often will wonder "Is this possible?" or "How would you do this?" Internet searches are the best way to find that answer. Micosoft's help is great for "how to" but less useful for "can you" type of inquiries.

Don't think you have to struggle alone, because chances are whatever you want to do has been done at some point by hundreds of others, some of whom asked how to do it and were told how in an online forum.

Now, keep in mind that web searches are probably becoming much less reliable these days thanks to AI and other crap, but there's still a lot of older help out there. (I'd say focus on results prior to about 2023 whenever possible.)

And if you're dealing with a newer function, the Microsoft support forums should still be a source of solid, reliable information on "can you" type of questions.

Okay, one more basic formula topic, and then we'll start working our way through actual functions.

# Operators and Calculation Order

Before we dive into functions, I want to cover operators that you can use in formulas, and how Excel goes through and performs more complex calculations.

Here is a table of the most common mathematical calculations:

|  | Operator | Example | Result | Function | Example |
|---|---|---|---|---|---|
| **Addition** | + | =3+2 | 5 | SUM | =SUM(3,2) |
| **Subtraction** | - | =3-2 | 1 | | |
| **Multiplication** | * | =3*2 | 6 | PRODUCT | =PRODUCT(3,2) |
| **Division** | / | =3/2 | 1.5 | | |
| **Exponential** | ^ | =3^2 | 9 | POWER | =POWER(3,2) |
| **Percent** | % | =50% | 0.5 | | |

The first column lists the type of calculation. The second column lists the "operator" you need to use to perform that calculation. (Operator is just a fancy way of saying the character you use.) The third column shows a formula that performs that calculation type. The fourth displays the result of the formula.

And then the last two columns show functions that can also be used for that type of calculation, and an example of them applied to the same numbers.

So, for example, for addition you use the plus sign ( + ) or the SUM function.

$$=3+2$$

returns the same result as

$$=SUM(3,2)$$

For subtraction you use the minus sign ( - ), for multiplication it's the asterisk ( * ) or PRODUCT function, and for division it's the forward slash ( / ).

To put one number to the power of another ,use the caret ( ^ ) or POWER function. To tell Excel to treat a number as a percentage, use the percent symbol (%).

You can also use greater than ( > ) or less than ( < ) operators when working with functions.

* * *

Within any given formula, Excel will perform calculations and complete functions in a set order. You can go to Help and look for "calculation operators and precedence" to see a full discussion of how this works, but here are the basics:

For the most part, Excel follows standard calculation rules and works from left to right.

Excel will start with all reference operators first. It will find anything that uses a colon or comma to reference a range of cells, and retrieve those values.

Next, it will apply any negatives that are in the formula.

Then percentages.

Then exponentials.

Then multiplication and division.

Then addition and subtraction.

Then any strings of text that need to be joined using the ampersand (&).

And finally, it will perform any equal to, greater than, or less than comparisons.

If you want a specific part of a formula calculated first before it is incorporated with the rest of the values in the formula, put parens around that part. So:

$$=2+3*5$$

will give a result of 17 because Excel multiplies 3 times 5 first and then goes back and adds 2. But

$$=(2+3)*5$$

will give a result of 25 because Excel does the part in parens, 2 + 3, first, and then multiplies that by 5.

As you can see, one misplaced paren and your results could be completely wrong. So always, always, always pay attention to what order things will happen in.

In the Formulas tab, there is an Evaluate Formula option in the Formula Auditing section. Use that to walk through a formula step-by-step, and see which calculations are being performed first.

We'll discuss that and other troubleshooting options at the end of this book. For now I want to dive in and start working with different functions.

# Top Functions to Learn

Before we start with specific functions, here are the five that I think you should learn no matter what:

### 1. SUM

I've already used this one more than once in examples in the introductory section. Pretty much anyone who is going to work with numbers in Excel will at some point want to add a range of numbers together. This function is how you do that.

### 2. TEXTJOIN

This one also does what it says. It joins strings of text together. You can also tell Excel what character(s) to use to separate each text string.

### 3. IFS

IFS lets you write formulas that return different results based on the data. Think of it as IF x, THEN y, ELSE z, but capable of much more complexity than that.

### 4. TRIM

TRIM removes extra spaces from text strings and is good for cleaning up messy data.

### 5. XLOOKUP

XLOOKUP will look for a value or the closest to that value in one columns, and then return that result or a value in another column.

These may not be the functions that you personally will use the most, but if you learn all five they will give you an understanding of how Excel functions work, and the variety of uses for them.

Now on to individual functions.

I've grouped them by type. We'll start with some Math & Trig and Statistical functions, then move on to Text functions, and then Date & Time functions. Finally, I'll round it out with a smattering of Logical, Lookup & Reference, and Information functions.

# The SUM Function

**Notation:** SUM(number1,[number2], …)

**Excel Definition:** Adds all the numbers in a range of cells.

The SUM function is probably the most-used function in Excel. There are ways to see the sum of values in cells without using it (like selecting the cells and looking in the bottom right corner of the workspace), and the AutoSum option can sometimes substitute for actually writing the formula yourself, but if there is one function you learn in Excel, this is the one.

SUM technically only requires one input.

$$=SUM(3)$$

will give you a result. But the reason for that is that you can sum millions of records with just one input. For example,

$$=SUM(D:F)$$

will sum all of the values in Columns D, E, and F.

As you can see in my first example above, it is possible to list the values directly in the function. For example:

$$=SUM(2,3,4)$$

will add 2, 3, and 4 and give a result of 9. But the real power of Excel comes with cell references, like I used above to refer to all of the values in three columns.

If you have multiple non-adjacent cell references that you want to sum, just separate them with commas. Like so:

$$=SUM(1:1,3:3,7:7)$$

which would sum all of the values in Rows 1, 3, and 7.

You can also use the SUM function to get around the fact that there is no function for subtracting a large number of values. The reason Excel doesn't have a function for subtraction is because with subtraction the order matters. Three minus two is different from two minus three. But if you have a starting value and everything else is being subtracted from that value, then you can use the SUM function to create a very simple formula. Like this:

$$=H16-SUM(A:A)$$

Here I am taking the value in Cell H16 and subtracting from it the values in the cells in Column A. The reason this works is because

$$=H16-A1-A2-A3$$

is equivalent mathematically to

$$=H16-(A1+A2+A3)$$

As I mentioned previously, you can sometimes use the AutoSum function to build your SUM function for you. Just be sure to check that it captures the right cell range. If there are gaps in your data it's liable to stop at the first gap it finds, so instead of summing A2:A100 it tries to sum A52:A100.

# The COUNT Function

**Notation:** COUNT(value1, [value2],…)

**Excel Definition:** Counts the number of cells in a range that contain numbers.

The COUNT function allows you to count how many cells within a selected range contain numbers. Excel sometimes refers to this as the Numerical Count option.

The "value1" input into the function is generally going to be a cell range. Note that since Excel stores dates as numbers, the COUNT function will count cells that contain dates as well.

Let's look at an example:

| | A | B |
|---|---|---|
| 1 | Visible Value | Type of Value |
| 2 | 12 | Number |
| 3 | 2-Jan | Date (1/2) |
| 4 | 0.5 | Number (1/2) |
| 5 | Ten | Text (Ten) |
| 6 | "1" | Text ("1") |
| 7 | 1 | Text ('1) |
| 8 | | |
| 9 | | COUNT |
| 10 | 3 | =COUNT(A2:A7) |
| 11 | | |
| 12 | | COUNTA |
| 13 | 6 | =COUNTA(A2:A7) |
| 14 | | |

In Cells A2 through A7 I have various values. A2 has the number 12, A3 had 1/2 which Excel turned into the date 2-Jan, A4 has '1/2 so it remained a number and shows as .5, A5 has the word Ten, A6 has the number 1 but in double quotes, and A7 has the number 1 but it was preceded by a single quote so is treated as text by Excel. You can see those value types in Column B.

In Cell A10, I used the formula

$$=COUNT(A2:A7)$$

The result is 3. Excel counted the two numbers in Cells A2 and A4 as well as the date in Cell A3. It did not count the text of a number nor did it count numbers preceded or surrounded by single or double quotes.

Let's look at another example:

| | E | F |
|---|---|---|
| 1 | Visible Value | Type of Value |
| 2 | 9 | Formula (+ sign) |
| 3 | 45305.50 | Formula (SUM) |
| 4 | 12452930.5 | Formula (TEXTJOIN) |
| 5 | | Blank |
| 6 | 1 day | Text (1 day) |
| 7 | | Formula (IFERROR blank) |
| 8 | | |
| 9 | | COUNT |
| 10 | 2 | =COUNT(E2:E7) |
| 11 | | |
| 12 | | COUNTA |
| 13 | 5 | =COUNTA(E2:E7) |
| 14 | | |

Here I've used a variety of formulas as well as included a blank cell and one that looks blank but is using a formula.

Cell E2 shows a value of 9 that was generated by using the plus sign to add two numbers together.

Cell E3 shows a value that was created by using the SUM function on three cells that had numbers in them.

Cell E4 looks like a number but it was created with the TEXTJOIN function so is in fact text.

Cell E5 is simply blank.

Cell E6 contains text that says 1 day.

Cell E7 looks like it's blank, but it was created using an IFERROR function that returns a result of "".

The COUNT function for Cells E2 through E7 returns a value of 2, for the values in Cells E2 and E3. Note that they are counted as numbers even though the actual contents in those cells are formulas that generated those numbers.

# The COUNTA Function

**Notation:** COUNTA(value1, [value2],…)

**Excel Definition:** Counts the number of cells in a range that are not empty.

Where COUNT is limited to numbers (including dates), the COUNTA function will count any cells in a range that "are not empty".

The result of the COUNTA function is what is displayed as the Count value in the bottom right corner when you select a range of cells in Excel.

Let's look at those two examples from the COUNT function again.

In the first example where every cell had something in it, the COUNTA function returns a value of six, because none of the cells are empty. Even though some are numbers, one is a date, and some are text, it counts them all.

| | A | B |
|---|---|---|
| 1 | **Visible Value** | **Type of Value** |
| 2 | 12 | Number |
| 3 | 2-Jan | Date (1/2) |
| 4 | 0.5 | Number (1/2) |
| 5 | Ten | Text (Ten) |
| 6 | "1" | Text ("1") |
| 7 | 1 | Text ('1) |
| 8 | | |
| 9 | | **COUNT** |
| 10 | 3 | =COUNT(A2:A7) |
| 11 | | |
| 12 | | **COUNTA** |
| 13 | 6 | =COUNTA(A2:A7) |
| 14 | | |

In the second example (on the opposite page) it returns a value of five. That's because of the two apparently blank cells, E5 and E7. Only one of them is truly blank, E5. Cell E7 looks blank but there is a formula in that cell that's currently displaying a blank result, so it gets counted.

It is important to understand this distinction, because there will be times where you want to write a formula that returns a blank value, but the COUNTA function is going to pick up those "blanks" as if there was something in that cell.

COUNT won't, though, because the result isn't a number or date.

This is also important to understand for situations where you use the COUNTA function to calculate something like an average, where you need to accurately count which cells have values in them.

Let's look at one final example with COUNTA:

Again we have a range of six cells.

Cells H2 and H6 have formulas that sum values in blank cells. Since the formulas used + or SUM which apply to numbers, they are both treated as numbers and captured by COUNT and COUNTA.

In Cells H3 and H7, I took the numbers in Cells H2 and H6 and pasted them back in as just their values. Those also were captured by COUNT and COUNTA.

So far, so good.

The tricky one is Cell H4, which is a copy and paste special – values version of a blank result (""). COUNTA counts that cell. It considers it to be "not empty". But if I look in the formula bar (see image above) I will see nothing there. Nothing to delete..

Note that for Cell H5, which was a paste special – values version of a truly blank cell, COUNTA ignored it just fine.

It's only the values that come from a null value that are problematic. To really clear a cell like that, you can either select the cell, and then use Clear Contents from the Editing section of the Home tab, or click on the cell and use Delete or Backspace.

# The AVERAGE Function

**Notation:** AVERAGE(number1, [number2],…)

**Excel Definition:** Returns the average (arithmetic mean) of its arguments, which can be numbers or names, arrays, or references that contain numbers.

Essentially the AVERAGE function combines the SUM and COUNT functions.

The way you calculate an average is you take a series of numbers, add them together, and then divide by the number of values you combined. So

$$=AVERAGE(A2:A7)$$

will return the same result as

$$=SUM(A2:A7)/COUNT(A2:A7)$$

Here is our data from before that we used for COUNT: but with AVERAGE applied:

| | A | B | C | D | E |
|---|---|---|---|---|---|
| 1 | Visible Value | Type of Value | | Column A Actual Number Value | |
| 2 | 12 | Number | | 12.00 | |
| 3 | 2-Jan | Date (1/2) | | 45293.00 | |
| 4 | 0.5 | Number (1/2) | | 0.50 | |
| 5 | Ten | Text (Ten) | | | |
| 6 | "1" | Text ("1") | | | |
| 7 | 1 | Text ('1) | | | |
| 8 | | | | SUM(A2:A7) | 45305.50 |
| 9 | | | | | |
| 10 | | AVERAGE | | COUNT(A2:A7) | 3 |
| 11 | 15101.8333 | =AVERAGE(A2:A7) | | D8/D10 | 15101.83333 |
| 12 | | | | | |
| 13 | | AVERAGEA | | COUNTA(A2:A7) | 6 |
| 14 | 7550.91667 | =AVERAGEA(A2:A7) | | D8/D13 | 7550.916667 |
| 15 | | | | | |

In Cells A2 through A7, we have the same values as before. We have three cells that have "numbers" in them and three that don't. (I put numbers in quotes since one of those numbers is in fact a date.)

Recall that COUNT returned a value of 3.

In Column D I have put the actual numbers that Excel is using for each one. That date, which displays as 2-Jan in Column A, is actually January 2, 2024 behind the scenes, which is stored by Excel as the number 45293.

(I'm on a PC. For PCs, Excel treats every date as a number counting from a start date of January 1, 1900 which has the value of 1.)

Which means to take an average over that range, Excel is going to add 45,293 to 12 and 0.5, to get a total of 45,305.50. For AVERAGE it will then divide that by 3, the COUNT result, giving the result of 15,101.833 shown in Cell A11.

\* \* \*

Now, here's where things get a little tricky. Remember that bottom corner where you can just select a range of cells and see calculations without using a formula? The average value that Excel shows there is the one for AVERAGE, but the count value is for COUNTA.

They do not match up.

Which is fine, really, because chances are that the type of average you will normally want is one that looks at numbers only, while the type of count you want is for every cell that has a value.

So there's a reason they did it that way. Just keep it in mind, so you know which one you're getting if you use that option.

This also brings up another issue.

What if you really wanted the average across all six cells, not only the ones that currently have numbers in them?

To use AVERAGE, you'd need to put a number in every cell, even if that number was zero.

\* \* \*

One final note: You may at times get a #DIV/0! Error message when you use AVERAGE on a range of cells. That happens when there are no numeric values in the range, so the COUNT is zero.

If that's because you haven't put in values yet, no problem, don't worry about it. If there are what you think are numbers there, no there aren't. Check your formatting.

# The AVERAGEA Function

**Notation:** AVERAGEA(value1, [value2],…)

**Excel Definition:** Returns the average (arithmetic mean) of its arguments, evaluating text and FALSE in arguments as 0; TRUE evaluates as 1. Arguments can be numbers, names, arrays, or references.

AVERAGEA is *not* the same as taking SUM and dividing it by COUNTA. That is because AVERAGEA will assign a value of 1 to TRUE values, whereas SUM does not.

Here is an example:

| | G | H | I | J | K |
|---|---|---|---|---|---|
| 1 | | | | Cells G3:G8 | |
| 2 | **Visible Value** | **Type of Value** | | **SUM** | 14 |
| 3 | 12 | Number | | | |
| 4 | 2 | Number | | **COUNT** | 2 |
| 5 | TRUE | Text (TRUE) | | **AVERAGE** | 7 |
| 6 | FALSE | Text (FALSE) | | =14/2 | 7 |
| 7 | TRUE | Formula TRUE | | | |
| 8 | FALSE | Formula FALSE | | **COUNTA** | 6 |
| 9 | | | | **AVERAGEA** | 2.666666667 |
| 10 | | | | =14/6 | 2.333333333 |
| 11 | | | | =16/6 | 2.666666667 |
| 12 | | | | | |

In Column G, there are two numbers and four TRUE or FALSE values. You can see in Cell K2 that SUM adds those values up to 14. But if we take the COUNTA value in Cell K8 and divide it by 14, the result is 2.33. The AVERAGE function, though, returns a value of 2.667.

That is because each TRUE value in a cell is counted as 1 by AVERAGEA, so it is using 16 as the summed value.

So you have to keep that distinction in mind when using AVERAGEA if there are TRUE or FALSE values in your data.

Now let's walk through an example that puts this to good use. Say that I want to know what percent of the class scored 90% or above on a test. I have 25 test results in Column O:

| | O | P | Q | R | S | T | U |
|---|---|---|---|---|---|---|---|
| 1 | **Score** | **90% or Above** | | | **AVERAGEA** | | |
| 2 | 85% | FALSE | =IF(O2>=0.9,TRUE(),FALSE()) | | 48% | =AVERAGEA(P2:P26) | |
| 3 | 92% | TRUE | | | | | |
| 4 | 96% | TRUE | | | 12 | =COUNTIF(P2:P26,TRUE) | |
| 5 | 100% | TRUE | | | 0.48 | =R4/25 | |
| 6 | 77% | FALSE | | | | | |
| 7 | 93% | TRUE | | | | | |
| 8 | 81% | FALSE | | | | | |
| 9 | 95% | TRUE | | | | | |
| 10 | 100% | TRUE | | | | | |
| 11 | 90% | TRUE | | | | | |
| 12 | 77% | FALSE | | | | | |
| 13 | 97% | TRUE | | | | | |
| 14 | 74% | FALSE | | | | | |
| 15 | 94% | TRUE | | | | | |
| 16 | 79% | FALSE | | | | | |
| 17 | 75% | FALSE | | | | | |
| 18 | 100% | TRUE | | | | | |
| 19 | 86% | FALSE | | | | | |
| 20 | 100% | TRUE | | | | | |
| 21 | 83% | FALSE | | | | | |
| 22 | 88% | FALSE | | | | | |
| 23 | 93% | TRUE | | | | | |
| 24 | 73% | FALSE | | | | | |
| 25 | 73% | FALSE | | | | | |
| 26 | 84% | FALSE | | | | | |
| 27 | | | | | | | |

I use an IF function, like I did in Column P, to identify those results that are 90 or above, and copy it down:

$$=IF(O2>=0.9,TRUE(),FALSE())$$

After that it's simple enough to use AVERAGEA on that range. Since TRUE is worth 1 and FALSE is worth 0, the AVERAGEA result is also a calculation of the percent of results that are 90 or above.

(To confirm that it worked, I used another function we'll cover later, COUNTIF, to count the number of values in Column P that were TRUE, and then I manually divided that result by 25 and got the same result. There's always more than one way to do something.)

If I'd wanted to see what percentage *weren't* 90% or above, I could either write the IF function differently to assign TRUE to values under .9, or I could subtract my AVERAGEA result from 1:

$$=1-AVERAGEA(P2:P26)$$

# The MIN Function

**Notation:** MIN(number1, [number2],…)

**Excel Definition:** Returns the smallest number in a set of values. Ignores logical values and text.

MIN, short for minimum, returns the smallest *numeric* value out of the list of values you give it.

Much like SUM, COUNT, and AVERAGE, the MIN function requires a "number" input, but what you're usually going to do is reference a range of cells.

Here are some examples:

| | A | B | C | D | E | F | G | H |
|---|---|---|---|---|---|---|---|---|
| 1 | Visible Value | Type of Value | | Visible Value | Type of Value | | Visible Value | Type of Value |
| 2 | 12 | Number | | 2 | Number | | -5 | Number |
| 3 | 2-Jan | Date (1/2) | | TRUE | Text (TRUE) | | 0.5 | Number |
| 4 | 0.5 | Number (1/2) | | FALSE | Text (FALSE) | | TRUE | Text (TRUE) |
| 5 | Ten | Text (Ten) | | | | | FALSE | Text (FALSE) |
| 6 | "1" | Text ("1") | | | | | | |
| 7 | 1 | Text ('1) | | | | | | |
| 8 | | | | | | | | |
| 9 | | MIN | | | MIN | | | MIN |
| 10 | 0.5 | =MIN(A2:A7) | | 2 | =MIN(D2:D4) | | -5 | =MIN(G2:G5) |
| 11 | | | | | | | | |
| 12 | | MINA | | | MINA | | | MINA |
| 13 | 0 | =MINA(A2:A7) | | 0 | =MINA(D2:D4) | | -5 | =MINA(G2:G5) |
| 14 | | | | | | | | |

In Column A, we have a range of values that includes three numeric values, 12 in Cell A2, the date January 2, 2024 in Cell A3 (which is also the number 45293), and the value 0.5 in Cell A4, as well as three text versions of numbers in Cells A5, A6, and A7.

The MIN function only looks at the numbers, so it returns a value of 0.5 for the minimum. You can see that in Cell A10.

The formula I used is in Cell B10:

$$=MIN(A2:A7)$$

In Column D, we have the number 2 in Cell D2, a TRUE value in Cell D3, and a FALSE value in Cell D4. Since MIN only looks at *numbers*, it returns a value of 2, which you can see in Cell D10 with the formula shown in Cell E10.

Column G has a negative value, -5, in Cell G2, a positive value, 0.5, in Cell G3, and then TRUE and FALSE in Cells G4 and G5.

This time MIN returns a value of -5, because that's the lowest numeric value in the range. You can see that in Cell G10 and the formula in Cell H10.

If MIN is referencing a range of only blank cells, it will return a value of zero, but if it is referencing a range of cells where some are blank and some have numbers, it will ignore the blank cells, and return the smallest numeric value in the range.

You can also set Excel to display the MIN result for a selected range of cells in the bottom right corner of your worksheet. The Min option is not available by default, though, so to do that, right-click where it says Count, Sum, and Average in the bottom corner, and then click on Minimum in the dropdown menu so that it's checked, like I have here:

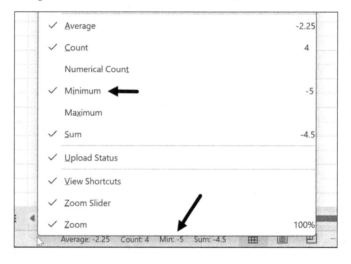

A Min value will only display in that section if at least one of the cells you select has a number in it.

# The MINA Function

**Notation:** MINA(value1, [value2],...)

**Excel Definition:** Returns the smallest value in a set of values. Does not ignore logical values and text.

The difference between MIN and MINA, is that MINA will include text values and logical values like TRUE or FALSE. Any text, formula with a blank result, or FALSE value in a cell, will be treated as a value of zero for the MINA function, while TRUE will be given the value of 1.

In the examples in the MIN chapter, there were also results displayed for MINA. It returned a different result for the values in Column A and Column D. Let's walk through why.

In Column A, the text values in Cells A5, A6, and A7 are assigned a value of zero by MINA, which makes that the smallest value.

In Column D, MINA assigns FALSE a value of 0 and TRUE a value of 1. That makes FALSE the smallest value in the range, and also returns a result of zero.

For Column G, both MIN and MINA return the same result, -5. That's because even though MINA assigns values to FALSE and TRUE, a negative number is less than either assigned value.

Just like with MIN, MINA will return a value of zero if it is referencing a range of blank cells. Unlike MIN, MINA will ignore blank cells if there is *any value* in the referenced range. So one cell in the range with a value of TRUE in it, will result in a minimum of 1 even if the rest of the cells in the range are blank.

Also, be careful with MINA, because if you have a formula in your cell range that returns a blank result, that will count as a value. So you could only see TRUE results in your cell range, but because the formula in that range returned a blank value, the MINA result would be zero. (You probably won't see this often, don't worry.)

Finally, neither MIN nor MINA can work if there is an error in the cell range. They'll return the error message instead of a value.

# The MAX Function

**Notation:** MAX(number1, [number2],…)

**Excel Definition:** Returns the largest value in a set of values. Ignores logical values and text.

The MAX function is the mirror of the MIN function, but instead of returning the smallest value in the range, it returns the largest.

Like MIN, MAX only looks at "numeric" values, which I put in quotes because dates are considered numbers by Excel, and chances are the number1 input that you provide the function will be a cell range not actual numbers.

Here are three examples of it applied to the same values we used for MIN and MINA:

| | A | B | C | D | E | F | G | H |
|---|---|---|---|---|---|---|---|---|
| 1 | Visible Value | Type of Value | | Visible Value | Type of Value | | Visible Value | Type of Value |
| 2 | 12 | Number | | 0.5 | Number | | -5 | Number |
| 3 | 2-Jan | Date (1/2) | | TRUE | Text (TRUE) | | 0.5 | Number |
| 4 | 0.5 | Number (1/2) | | FALSE | Text (FALSE) | | TRUE | Text (TRUE) |
| 5 | Ten | Text (Ten) | | | | | FALSE | Text (FALSE) |
| 6 | "1" | Text ("1") | | | | | | |
| 7 | 1 | Text ('1) | | | | | | |
| 8 | | | | | | | | |
| 9 | | MAX | | | MAX | | | MAX |
| 10 | 45293 | =MAX(A2:A7) | | 0.5 | =MAX(D2:D4) | | 0.5 | =MAX(G2:G5) |
| 11 | | | | | | | | |
| 12 | | MAXA | | | MAXA | | | MAXA |
| 13 | 45293 | =MAXA(A2:A7) | | 1 | =MAXA(D2:D4) | | 1 | =MAXA(G2:G5) |
| 14 | | | | | | | | |

You can see the formula used for Column A's values in Cell B10:

=MAX(A2:A7)

Because Column A has that date value, the numeric equivalent, 45,293, is the largest value in that range.

In Column D there is only one numeric value, 0.5, so that is the value that MAX returns.

In Column G there are two numeric values, 0.5 and -5, and MAX returns the value 0.5 because it is the larger of the two numbers.

Just like MIN, MAX will return a value of zero for blank cell ranges or cell ranges that don't have any numbers in them. And if there is an error message in the range, it will return the error message.

You can also set Excel to show the Max value of a selected range of cells in the bottom right corner of the worksheet.

# The MAXA Function

**Notation:** MAXA(value1, [value2],…)

**Excel Definition:** Returns the largest value in a set of values. Does not ignore logical values and text.

The MAXA function is the counterpart to MINA. It treats text and TRUE or FALSE values the same way, assigning a value of zero to text or FALSE values, and a value of one to TRUE values.

In the last chapter, you can see that I also applied MAXA to those values.

In Column A, MAXA returns the value of 45,293 because even assigning a value to the text entries there doesn't change that the date value is the largest value in that range.

In Column D, MAXA returns a different result from MAX. That's because TRUE is assigned a value of 1, which makes it the largest value in the range.

Same for Column G. MAXA returns a different result because TRUE, when assigned a value of 1, is the largest value in the range.

As with MAX, MAXA will return an error message if there's an error in the referenced range. It will also return a value of zero for a range of blank cells, but will ignore blank cells if there is any value in any cell in the referenced range of cells.

MAXA also has the issue MINA does, where it will treat a cell with a formula that returns a blank result as a zero, which means it can return a result you don't expect to see if you're dealing with negative numbers in your other cells. You might see − 5, -3, -2, and expect the MAXA result to be -2, but if there's a formula there with a blank result, you'll get a value of 0 as your maximum. Just something to keep in mind if things aren't working the way you think they "should".

# The SMALL Function

**Notation:** SMALL(array, k)

**Excel Definition:** Returns the k-th smallest value in a data set. For example, the fifth smallest number.

What the SMALL function does is it looks at a range of values, puts them in order from smallest to largest, and then pulls for you the k-th smallest value.

I honestly don't use the SMALL function that much, but it is a handy one to know if you happen to need what it provides. Its counterpart, which is discussed in the next chapter, is the LARGE function.

This is the first function we've covered that *requires* more than one input. It's a pretty basic one, so nice for demonstrating a few things.

Look at the cell notation above, SMALL(array,k). That means the SMALL function requires that you provide two separate inputs, the range of cells (i.e. array) that contain your values, and then a number that represents the position you want to pull from. For example, entering 1 for your k-value will give you the smallest number in the range.

Both inputs are required for this function to work. SMALL will give you a "too few arguments entered" error if you fail to provide a value for k. It will give you a #NUM! error if you put a comma but leave the k-value blank.

Now let's look at a few examples of SMALL applied to a range of values.

On the next page, in Column A I have fifteen randomly-generated numbers that are not sorted. It makes it a little challenging to find the smallest number, doesn't it? It would be even more challenging to find the third or seventh smallest. Imagine if this were 1,000 entries instead of 15.

Yikes!

But that's what SMALL is for.

| | A | B | C | D | E | F |
|---|---|---|---|---|---|---|
| 1 | **Values** | | | | | |
| 2 | 670 | | **k-value** | **SMALL** | **k-smallest Result** | |
| 3 | 353 | | 1 | =SMALL(A:A,C3) | 113 | |
| 4 | 722 | | 3 | =SMALL(A:A,C4) | 196 | |
| 5 | 196 | | 7 | =SMALL(A:A,C5) | 528 | |
| 6 | 572 | | 15 | =SMALL(A:A,C6) | 998 | |
| 7 | 528 | | | | | |
| 8 | 693 | | **k-value** | **LARGE** | **k-largest Result** | |
| 9 | 198 | | 1 | =LARGE(A:A,C9) | 998 | |
| 10 | 998 | | 3 | =LARGE(A:A,C10) | 722 | |
| 11 | 113 | | 7 | =LARGE(A:A,C11) | 662 | |
| 12 | 697 | | 15 | =LARGE(A:A,C12) | 113 | |
| 13 | 456 | | | | | |
| 14 | 150 | | | | | |
| 15 | 958 | | | | | |
| 16 | 662 | | | | | |
| 17 | | | | | | |

In Cells C3 through C6, I have four k-values: 1, 3, 7, and 15. That will give me the smallest number, the third smallest, the seventh smallest, and, since I have fifteen values, my largest.

I wrote a formula in Cell D3 that uses a column reference for my array and a cell reference for the k-value. This says, look at all the values in Column A and take the k-th smallest value where k is in Cell C3:

$$=SMALL(A:A,C3)$$

Writing it that way lets me copy the formula to Cells D4 through D6 without having to rewrite it. Excel automatically adjusts the k-value cell reference for me.

Note, too, that by using a cell reference in my formula, and showing the k-values in that table, I am also making my inputs visible, which is a data best practice. Anyone can quickly see from that table that the values in Column E are meant to return the first, third, seventh, and fifteenth smallest values.

One little bonus trick before we move on. Since we already learned COUNT, you can combine SMALL and COUNT together to return the largest value in the range for you using:

$$=SMALL(A:A,COUNT(A:A))$$

That sets the k value to whatever the COUNT of numeric values in Column A is, and will continue to work no matter the number of numeric values in Column A. It's a little twisty because you have to use the SMALL function to get the largest value, but it works..

# The LARGE Function

**Notation:** LARGE(array, k)

**Excel Definition:** Returns the k-th largest value in a data set. For example, the fifth largest number.

As I mentioned in the last chapter, the SMALL function and the LARGE function are counterparts of one another. In the screenshot on the opposite page you can see formulas that use the LARGE function in Cells D9 through D12.

I once more used cell references to make my life easy, so the first formula there is:

=LARGE(A:A,C9)

But to get the largest value in Column A, you could also use:

=LARGE(A:A,1)

To get the smallest value in Column A when you don't know how many numbers you're dealing with, you could use

=LARGE(A:A,COUNT(A:A))

Or, since we know there are 15 values, you could use:

=LARGE(A:A,15)

# The ROUND Function

**Notation:** ROUND(number, num_digits)

**Excel Definition:** Rounds a number to a specified number of digits.

The ROUND function does what you think it would, it rounds numbers.

Note that the ROUND function is another one that requires two inputs. The first input is the number that you want to round. That can be, and usually will be, a cell reference.

The second input is the number of digits you want to round to. This should be a whole number.

If it isn't a whole number, Excel will just ignore any decimal places, so using 2.73 for num_digits will be treated as 2.

A num_digits value of 0 will return a number with no decimal places. A positive num_digits value will return a number with that number of decimal places. A negative num_digits value will return a number rounded to the nearest tens, hundreds, thousands, etc.

For example, 12,345 can be rounded to 12,000 using:

$$=ROUND(12345,-3)$$

Note that the num_digits here is -3.

It is possible to format a number using a format like Currency or Accounting to make it look like you've rounded it to two decimal places, but when you use a number formatted that way in a formula, Excel will still use the original number. ROUND, on the other hand, transforms a number to truly only have the specified number of digits.

Okay. So, how does Excel round numbers?

It looks at the digit *one past* where you want to round to. If that digit is 0 through 4, it leaves the number you want to round to alone, and drops everything past that point. If the number is 5 through 9, it increases the number you want to round to by one, and also drops everything past that point.

If you're rounding to the left of the decimal place, it puts in zeroes to replace the numbers that were dropped..

Let's look at some examples:

| | A | B | C | |
|---|---|---|---|---|
| 1 | **Value** | **Digits to Round** | **ROUND** | |
| 2 | 123.123 | 2 | 123.12 | |
| 3 | 123.123 | 0 | 123 | |
| 4 | 123.123 | -2 | 100 | |
| 6 | 567.567 | 2 | 567.57 | |
| 7 | 567.567 | 0 | 568 | |
| 8 | 567.567 | -2 | 600 | |
| 9 | | | | |
| 10 | **Formula In Row 2:** | | =ROUND(A2,B2) | |
| 11 | | | | |

Here is a table with numbers in Column A. Rows 2 through 4 use the number 123.123 (so things should always round down) and Rows 6 through 8 use the number 567.567 (so things should always round up).

Because I'm lazy, I put the various num_digits values I wanted to work with in Column B. That let me write a formula in Cell C2 that I could then just copy to the other cells in Column C.

That formula was:

=ROUND(A2,B2)

Which is saying, "Take the value in Cell A2 (which is 123.123) and round it by the number of digits in Cell B2 (which is 2)."

In Column C you can see what the ROUND function does with each combination of the value in Column A and the num_digits in Column B.

For 2 digits, so Rows 2 and 6, 123.123 becomes 123.12 and 567.567 becomes 567.57. Both times, Excel went to the digit one past the second digit after the decimal, and then either rounded down (for a 3) or rounded up (for a 7).

For 0 digits, so Rows 3 and 7, 123.123 becomes 123 and 567.567 becomes 568. Again, Excel went to the first digit after the specified location, and then either rounded down (for a 1) or rounded up (for a 5).

For -2 digits, so Rows 4 and 8, 123.123 becomes 100 and 567.567 becomes 600. This one is a little harder for me to wrap my head around, but once more, Excel goes to the digit to the right of where we specified, so the 2 for 123.123 and the 6 for 567.567, and then rounds up or down accordingly.

If you want to force Excel's hand, there are two other functions, ROUNDUP and ROUNDDOWN, which will force Excel to always round up or always round down. Here you can see how those would work on these same numbers:

| | A | B | C | D | E |
|---|---|---|---|---|---|
| 1 | Value | Digits to Round | ROUND | ROUNDUP | ROUNDDOWN |
| 2 | 123.123 | 2 | 123.12 | 123.13 | 123.12 |
| 3 | 123.123 | 0 | 123 | 124 | 123 |
| 4 | 123.123 | -2 | 100 | 200 | 100 |
| 6 | 567.567 | 2 | 567.57 | 567.57 | 567.56 |
| 7 | 567.567 | 0 | 568 | 568 | 567 |
| 8 | 567.567 | -2 | 600 | 600 | 500 |
| 9 | | | | | |
| 10 | Formula In Row 2: | | =ROUND(A2,B2) | =ROUNDUP(A2,B2) | =ROUNDDOWN(A2,B2) |
| 11 | | | | | |

Column D shows what happens when you use ROUNDUP. Column E shows what happens when you use ROUNDDOWN.

I used to do this for budgeting and it worked well. I would round all of my expenses up to the nearest five or ten dollars, and round all of my income down. It meant I always had a little extra I hadn't planned on. But in most situations, you'll want to use ROUND because it balances out over a lot of values, and keeps you close to the actual result.

Okay. Now on to a really simple one, absolute value.

# The ABS Function

**Notation:** ABS(number)

**Excel Definition:** Returns the absolute value of a number, a number without its sign.

As the definition says, ABS gives you the absolute value of a number. Interestingly enough, it works on numbers that are stored as text even though a function like SUM won't.

It only takes one input, the number (or cell reference for the number, more like).

For example:

$$=ABS(A1)$$

would take whatever value is in Cell A1, and turn it into a positive number.

When I use ABS, I usually paste special-values after I'm done. Since ABS is a function, if you delete the cell that was being referenced by it, you will get a #REF! error. The only way to remove the original values but keep your absolute value result is to convert that result from formulas to values.

You may be wondering when you would use this. One example I have, is when I'm looking at financials and I have positive values of money coming in and negative values going out. To easily see the largest transactions, whether in or out, I will create a column with ABS applied to the sum of my Money In and Money Out columns.

$$=ABS(A1+B1)$$

I can then sort or filter on that column to get the largest transactions. If I didn't do that, the largest money out would be at the opposite end of the list from the largest money in if the data is sorted. And if I used a filter, I'd need to use a custom filter to show the largest negative and positive values at the same time. Using ABS is easier.

# The RANDBETWEEN Function

**Notation:** RANDBETWEEN(bottom, top)

**Excel Definition:** Returns a random number between the numbers you specify.

In writing this book, I have used RANDBETWEEN more times than I can count. Because what it does is lets you quickly and easily generate a series of whole numbers that fall within the range you specify. So that range of numbers for MIN and MAX? Generated by RANDBETWEEN. And the numbers used for SMALL and LARGE? Same.

RANDBETWEEN takes two inputs, the lowest possible number in the range, and the highest possible number in the range.

For example, if I want random numbers between 65 and 100, I would use:

=RANDBETWEEN(65,100)

and then copy that formula down however many rows I need.

Now, in that case, I wanted percentage values. So I had to write it as:

=RANDBETWEEN(65,100)/100

because RANDBETWEEN only generates whole number values.

RANDBETWEEN can also generate negative numbers.

For example,

=RANDBETWEEN(-100,100)

will generate random whole numbers between negative one hundred and positive one hundred.

It is possible that a value will repeat if you have a limited range of numbers. Each cell is its own formula. So each cell is randomly pulling a value from the range you gave it, independent of the other cells using that formula.

There is another function, RAND, that is similar to RANDBETWEEN, but what it returns is a random decimal value greater than 0 and less than 1 that is evenly distributed.

I never use it because I think I get the same result with something like:

$$=\text{RANDBETWEEN}(0,1000000)/1000000$$

If you do use RAND, it does not require any inputs. You just write it and then follow it with empty parens. For another example of a function that works like that, see the TODAY function, because I can't actually write the RAND function here. If I do, Word will turn it into a block of random text.

One final warning. The numbers you generate with RAND or RANDBETWEEN are *not static*. Every time you hit F9, use another formula, add text to a cell and hit Enter, etc., all of your randomly-generated values will generate again, and *you can't get the old numbers back*.

Undo does not work.

So if you are generating a list of random numbers that you want to do something with, turn them into fixed values before you do anything else.

I usually use paste special-values, but if you need to lock your result down immediately, type your formula in like normal, and then use F9 instead of Enter when you're done, and before you leave that cell.

That will use your formula to perform the calculation and also immediately convert the cell contents to the result. Use Enter, Tab, or click away to then leave the cell. (If you use Esc it will revert to the formula.)

To apply the F9 trick to an existing cell with a formula, click into the formula bar, use F2 after clicking on that cell or double-click on the cell, and then use F9.

Now let's discuss a new-to-me function, RANDARRAY, which is going to be our first array function.

# The RANDARRAY Function

**Notation:** RANDARRAY([rows],[columns],[min],[max],[integer])

**Excel Definition:** Returns an array of random numbers.

One of the reasons I like writing these books is because it forces me to think through the various tools I use when working in Excel, and dig for better answers.

For example, just now when I was writing the RANDBETWEEN chapter, I thought, "I wonder if Excel has a function for generating a *range* of random numbers instead of doing it just one cell at a time like I do with RANDBETWEEN."

The answer was yes, RANDARRAY.

First off, let me tell you what an array function is. It's a function that can return results in more than one cell at a time. We haven't dealt with one of these yet. They're fairly new to Excel. I think it's only been the last three or four versions of Excel that have had them. The way they work has also changed over time. This is a book for Excel 2024, so I'm not going to get into how they used to work, but keep that in mind if you ever have to use an older version of Excel. You may have RANDARRAY available, but need to go to the Help function to see how to use it.

Okay. So.

First thing to note with RANDARRAY: Every single input to the function is listed in brackets, which means they are all optional. You can just write

=RANDARRAY()

and you will get a result. It will be the same result as if you'd used RAND: One cell with a decimal value between 0 and 1.

But RANDARRAY can do so much more than that.

The first input to the function is rows. The default value is 1. You can leave this input blank if you want one row of results. Or you can put a positive whole number which will tell Excel how many rows you want to populate with random values.

The second input is columns. It works the same as rows. Default is 1. If you only want one column of values, leave it blank. Otherwise put a positive whole number for the number of columns you want.

If you try to use a 0 for rows or columns, you will get a #CALC! error. If you try to use a negative value you will get a VALUE! error. So you either have to leave the inputs blank, or you have to put a positive whole number. (You can technically put a decimal, like 2.5, but Excel is just going to take the whole number portion and ignore the rest.)

The next two inputs to RANDARRY are min and max. This is the number range you want Excel to use when generating your random numbers. Leave those values blank and you'll get results between 0 and 1.

The final input, integer, is a TRUE/FALSE input. The default is FALSE, or 0, which will return decimal results. Put TRUE here (or the value 1) to get only integer results.

To use the default value for any input, just skip putting a value, and use a comma to indicate you're providing the next input. Here, for example, I have a RANDARRAY formula that will create a 2 by 2 grid of 0 and 1 values:

$$=RANDARRAY(2,2,,,1)$$

I used 2 for rows, 2 for columns, but then left min and max blank so that meant my range was going to be between 0 and 1. But then I put 1, TRUE, for my last input, which limited the result to whole numbers. That means in each of the four cells where Excel returns a value, the value will either be 1 or 0.

Here is another example:

$$=RANDARRAY(,4,1,10,TRUE)$$

This tells Excel to generate whole number values between 1 and 10 in four cells in a single row. Here is the result when the formula is in Cell A1:

| A1 | | | | $f_x$ | =RANDARRAY(,4,1,10,TRUE) | | |
|---|---|---|---|---|---|---|---|
| | A | B | C | D | E | F |
| 1 | 8 | 7 | 7 | 8 | | |
| 2 | | | | | | |
| 3 | | | | | | |
| 4 | | | | | | |

A few more things to note about working with an array formula.

The formula goes in the first cell of the range where you want your values. So above, even though it gave me values in Cells A1 through D1, the formula I entered was entered into Cell A1.

When you're clicked away from cells that contain the results of an array formula, they look perfectly normal. It's only when you click onto them that you can see that the values were generated as part of an array function.

As you can see in the screenshot above, Excel puts a border around all of the cells that were populated using the array formula when you click on any cell in that range.

To edit an array formula, go to the top left cell of the range. The formula will show in the formula bar for any of the cells in the range, but will be grayed out for all but that top left cell.

Another thing to know about array functions is that they need enough room to work. You can't use an array function that takes up five rows by five columns if you already have text or values in that space. You'll get a #SPILL! error if there isn't enough room.

Every time you see #SPILL! that means that you are using an array function, and that the function doesn't have enough room to display its results. Either clear the contents of the cells that are blocking the formula, or move the formula to a cell where it has enough room. With RANDARRAY, you could also edit the formula to take up less space.

One more example before we move on. Here I nested RANDARRAY with decimal places within a ROUND function to generate a five-by-five table of currency values between 1 and 100:

$$=ROUND(RANDARRAY(5,5,1,100,FALSE),2)$$

This is what the result looks like:

| C3 | | fx | =ROUND(RANDARRAY(5,5,1,100,FALSE),2) | | | |
|---|---|---|---|---|---|---|
| | A | B | C | D | E | F | G |
| 1 | 71.25 | 37.72 | 5.06 | 53.69 | 75.44 | |
| 2 | 75.8 | 80.69 | 31.34 | 5.4 | 86.56 | |
| 3 | 31.01 | 10.45 | 23.9 | 3.63 | 87.18 | |
| 4 | 52.2 | 78.34 | 1.28 | 56.33 | 18.71 | |
| 5 | 35.71 | 24.09 | 63.54 | 68 | 79.79 | |

Note that even though I am clicked into Cell C3, the formula you see is the one that was entered into Cell A1. Also, that the cells that are the result of the formula all have a border around the perimeter. And that the formula in the formula bar is grayed out because Cell C3 contains results from the formula, but not the formula itself.

One final note. RANDARRAY is a random-number-generating function, so be sure to lock down your values before you use your random numbers for any sort of calculation or demonstration that requires the numbers to stay fixed.

As I said before, I generally use paste special-values, but F9 did lock in the values for me here just in a unique way. It listed the values that were generated within a set of curly brackets in the first cell of the range. So =RANDARRAY(2,2,1,10,1) became ={9,4;2,8} and displayed the values 9, 4, 2, and 8 in a 2 by 2 range of cells.

# The SUMIFS Function

**Notation:** SUMIFS(sum_range, criteria_range1, criteria1, …)

**Excel Definition:** Adds the cells specified by a given set of conditions or criteria.

This is one of my favorite functions. I use it all the time. What SUMIFS does is lets you apply SUM to a range of values if certain criteria are met. There is an older function, SUMIF, that let you do this for one single criteria, but if you master SUMIFS, you won't need it.

Okay, so let's look at the required inputs.

The first input is the range of cells where the values you want to add up are located.

The second input is the first range of cells that contain information you want to evaluate. It can be the same range of cells as the ones you want to sum. Later, for example, I have a formula for determining the total value of purchases over $100.

The third input is your criteria you want to apply to that range of cells.

For this function that … at the end is important to understand. Because if you keep going, you need to actually add two additional inputs at a time. The next input you'd put there is the *second* range of cells that you want to evaluate. But you'd also then need to provide a fifth input, which is the criteria to use on that second range of cells.

This is what that would look like written out in notation format:

SUMIFS(sum_range, criteria_range1, criteria1, criteria_range2, criteria2,…)

The maximum number of criteria you can have is 127, although why you would ever want to do that, I do not know. That would be way too prone to error in my opinion.

Speaking of errors. If your cell ranges are not the same size for each range input (sum_range and each criteria_range), you will get a #VALUE! error. Excel needs to know what to match up.

I've only ever used SUMIFS (or any of the similar functions that we'll discuss next) with a table of data where my input ranges were in columns. But I did just try it with rows, and that worked, too. You can also use something like a 2x3 cell range, but all of your range inputs would then need to be 2x3 as well. The ranges always have to match up.

Your criteria can look at numeric values, dates, or text. You can also combine different types of criteria in the same function.

For example, I can have Excel sum transactions that occurred in 2024 (a date criteria), were over $100 (a number criteria), and involved customers in Alaska (a text criteria).

Let's now talk about how to write each of those properly.

For a number, you can either just write the number (22) or use quote marks around the number ("22").

For a greater than ( > ), less than ( < ), greater than or equal to ( >= ), or less than or equal to ( <= ) criteria, you need to put the whole expression in quotes. So greater than or equal to 22, would be ">=22" in that part of the function.

To evaluate dates, you also need to put them in quotes. So "7/23/2020" or "7/23/20" both work. If all else fails, convert the date you want to a number (44035 in this case), and write it that way, but you shouldn't have to do that.

It is possible to combine dates with the greater than and less than symbols as well. For example using ">5/1/2020" would look for any entry in the range after May 1, 2020.

You can also use cell references if the value you want is in a cell. (This is very useful for something like counting the number of sales per state. Create a list of all state abbreviations, write a formula that references the first entry in that list, use fixed cell references for your table or reference the entire column, and then just copy that formula down for all the states.)

To use greater than, less than, etc. with a cell reference, you have to write it as ">"& and then the cell reference. So

$$">"\&G25$$

would be how you write greater than the value in Cell G25.

To evaluate text, put it in quotes. So, "Alaska" would look for entries in that cell range for Alaska.

With text you can also use wildcards. An asterisk ( * ) represents any number of characters or spaces. So if I write

$$"*e*"$$

as my criteria, that would look for any entry that contains the letter e.

If I instead looked for

$$"e*"$$

that would look for any entry that *starts* with the letter e. And if I used

$$"*e"$$

that would look for any entry that *ends* with the letter e.

The other available wildcard is the question mark ( ? ), which represents one single character, including a single space.

So if I looked for

"??e"

that would return any three-letter entry that ends in e.

But keep in mind that each question mark is a character/space so "??e" would not capture the entry "be" since it is only two letters.

Also. If you ever want to use text that includes an actual asterisk or a question mark in your criteria, precede the asterisk or question mark with a tilde ( ~ ).

Okay. Time to look at some examples. Here is our data:

| | A | B | C | D | E |
|---|---|---|---|---|---|
| 1 | Date | Customer Name | Product | Units | Total Cost |
| 2 | 2/6/2020 | Lee | Widget | 14 | $ 31.50 |
| 3 | 2/25/2020 | Morales | Whatchamacallit | 3 | $ 33.75 |
| 4 | 4/1/2020 | Jones | Widget | 8 | $ 18.00 |
| 5 | 4/7/2020 | Jones | Whatchamacallit | 11 | $ 123.75 |
| 6 | 4/25/2020 | Phong | Whatsit | 11 | $ 14.85 |
| 7 | 4/28/2020 | Gutierrez | Widget | 9 | $ 20.25 |
| 8 | 5/2/2020 | Holsen | Whatchamacallit | 24 | $ 270.00 |
| 9 | 5/4/2020 | Morales | Whatsit | 15 | $ 20.25 |
| 10 | 5/6/2020 | Gutierrez | Whatsit | 1 | $ 1.35 |
| 11 | 5/26/2020 | Lee | Whatchamacallit | 3 | $ 33.75 |
| 12 | 6/10/2020 | Smith | Whatchamacallit | 4 | $ 9.00 |
| 13 | 6/12/2020 | Smith | Whatsit | 2 | $ 2.70 |
| 14 | 7/11/2020 | Holsen | Widget | 6 | $ 13.50 |
| 15 | 7/18/2020 | Phong | Whatchamacallit | 9 | $ 101.25 |
| 16 | 7/23/2020 | Fromer | Whatsit | 11 | $ 14.85 |
| 17 | | | | | |

We have date of transaction, customer last name, product, units bought, and total cost.

I want to answer the following questions using this data:

1. How much did customer Lee spend?

2. How much did customer Lee spend on or after May 1, 2020?

3. What was the total value of purchases over $100?

4. How many What-type products did customer Smith purchase?

Take a moment and think about how you'd do that. And then look here at how I did it:

| Question | Formula | Result |
|---|---|---|
| How much did customer Lee spend? | =SUMIFS(E2:E16,B2:B16,"Lee") | $ 65.25 |
| How much did customer Lee spend on or after May 1, 2020? | =SUMIFS(E2:E16,B2:B16,"Lee",A2:A16,">=5/1/2020") | $ 33.75 |
| What was the total value of purchases over $100? | =SUMIFS(E2:E16,E2:E16,">100") | $ 495.00 |
| How many What-type products did customer Smith purchase? | =SUMIFS(D2:D16,C2:C16,"What*",B2:B16,"Smith") | 6 |

The first question was "How much did customer Lee spend?" Which means we want to sum the cost column, and we have one criteria to apply, that the customer last name be Lee.

Here that is:

$$=SUMIFS(E2:E16,B2:B16,"Lee")$$

Note here that our criteria was text, so Lee is in quotes.

The next question takes that first example and limits it with a second criteria to purchases made on or after May 1, 2020. Adding that to our formula we get:

$$=SUMIFS(E2:E16,B2:B16,"Lee",A2:A16,">=5/1/2020")$$

Note that the >= and the date itself are all in quotes together.

Now let's look at the third question, "What was the total value of purchases over $100?" With this one, the criteria range and the sum range are the same:

$$=SUMIFS(E2:E16,E2:E16,">100")$$

It also uses a greater than symbol with a number, so both have to be included in quotes. Another option would be:

$$=SUMIFS(E2:E16,E2:E16,">"\&100)$$

where we join the greater than symbol to the number using an ampersand.

The fourth question is "How many what-type products did customer Smith purchase?"

To solve this one, we have to think about our product types. We have Whatsits, Widgets, and Whatchamacallits. Two of those are "what-type" products, Whatsits and Whatchamacallits.

The simplest solution is to use the wildcard asterisk character to get our answer:

$$=SUMIFS(D2:D16,C2:C16,"What*",B2:B16,"Smith")$$

By using "What*" I captured both products. (Note that Excel is not case-sensitive with text criteria so it views what and What as the same.)

Another option would be:

$$=SUM(SUMIFS(D2:D16,C2:C16,\{"Whatsit","Whatchamacallit"\},B2:B16,"Smith"))$$

Note that I used curly brackets to create a list for that particular input. And that because the list didn't use the plural of each product name, I had to be careful to use "Whatsit" instead of "Whatsits" and "Whatchamacallit" instead of "Whatchamacallits".

Also, it required SUM around the SUMIFS function, because otherwise it returns separate results in separate cells for Whatsit and Whatchamacallit.

Finally, note that this last example used a different sum range (Column D), because we were adding up units this time rather than amount made.

One final thought, I always like to test things like this on on a small range of my data where I can also manually compute the answer. That lets me confirm that the result my formula returns is what I'd expect.

One mistake I often make when initially writing a formula or filter or anything else involving numbers, is that I will write it as "greater than" or "less than" when what I really want is "greater than or equal to" or "less than or equal to". So I always try to test my edge cases. For example, with the $100 or more question, I'd use fake data that included values of 99.99, 100, and 100.01 to see if the result matched my expectations.

The other things I check for if I get an error message or my formula isn't working as expected, is that my quotes, commas, and cell ranges are where and what they should be.

# The COUNTIFS Function

**Notation:** COUNTIFS(criteria_range1, criteria1, …)

**Excel Definition:** Counts the number of cells specified by a given set of conditions or criteria.

Where SUMIFS sums values based on the criteria you give it, COUNTIFS counts them. Despite the name, the type of count function used here is COUNTA, which, if you recall, counts more than just numbers. (This is good, actually, I just mention it lest there be confusion.)

Note that since COUNTIFS is just counting results, it doesn't require that first input that SUMIFS does. It jumps right into the criteria ranges.

Also, just like SUMIFS has SUMIF, there is a COUNTIF function that can be used for one criteria. You can actually turn a COUNTIF function into a COUNTIFS function just by adding an S to the function name. (You can't do this with SUMIF and SUMIFS because the inputs are in a different order.)

In terms of building a COUNTIFS function, most of what you need to know was already discussed in the SUMIFS chapter. They handle criteria in the exact same way. So let's just dive in and walk through some questions we can answer with COUNTIFS.

Using the same data from the SUMIFS chapter, how would you answer the following questions:

1. How many transactions were there for customer Phong?

2. How many purchases did customer Phong make of Whatchamacallits?

3. How many purchases of more than ten units were made in April 2020?

4. How many purchases of Widgets and Whatsits were made?

Let's start with the first one: "How many transactions were there for customer Phong?" You just need Column B for this one, right?

If you did this manually, you would look down Column B, and every time it says "Phong", you would count that entry. Written as a formula it looks like this:

=COUNTIFS(B:B,"Phong")

The next question, "How many purchases of Whatchamacallits did customer Phong make?" takes that initial count but refines it to only transactions in Whatchamacallits.

That requires two pieces of information, customer name and product. As a formula it looks like this:

=COUNTIFS(B:B,"Phong",C:C,"Whatchamacallit")

(Note here that I'm using the entire columns for my cell ranges. I have nothing below my data table, so I can get away with that.)

The next question is a bit trickier: "How many purchases of more than ten units were made in April 2020?"

The first part is easy enough, it's just using the Units column and looking for any value greater than ten. But stop and think about what it means to be in April 2020. Clearly you need to use the Date column, but how would you write that?

Here's what I ended up doing:

=COUNTIFS(D:D,">10",A:A,">=4/1/2020",A:A,"<5/1/20")

I used two criteria on the same column. The date needed to be on or after April 1, 2020, that's the first criteria I used, and also before May 1, 2020, that's the second criteria I used.

Was is the most elegant and streamlined solution? Maybe not. But on something simple like this, "if it works, it works" is a good approach to take. When you're dealing with 15 rows of data you can be a bit clunky.

Okay. Final one: How many purchases of Widgets and Whatsits were made?

We can't use the wildcard symbol like we did in the last chapter, so we need to come up with another approach. This is the one I came up with:

=COUNTIFS(C:C,"Widget")+COUNTIFS(C:C,"Whatsit")

And it worked.

But as you may recall from the SUMIFS chapter, I could have also used:

=SUM(COUNTIFS(C:C,{"Widget","Whatsit"}))

Let's explore what happens when I don't surround that with SUM.

On the next page is a screenshot of a table I created with my product names in Column H. In Cell I2, I put the following formula:

=COUNTIFS(C:C,H2:H4)

| I2 | ∨ : ✕ ✓ *fx* | =COUNTIFS(C:C,H2:H4) | ← Formula |

| | H | I | J |
| --- | --- | --- | --- |
| 1 | **Product** | **Count of Sales** | |
| 2 | Whatsit | 5 | |
| 3 | Widget | 4 | |
| 4 | Whatchamacallit | 6 | |
| 5 | | | |
| 6 | | | |

**Array Result**

That returns an array result. Excel filled Cells I2 through I4 with the count for each product type itself.

I didn't have to copy a formula to get this result, Excel just did it.

Pretty interesting, huh?

# The AVERAGEIFS Function

**Notation:** AVERAGEIFS(average_range, criteria_range1, criteria1, …)

**Excel Definition:** Finds average (arithmetic mean) for the cells specified by a given set of conditions or criteria.

AVERAGEIFS works much like SUMIFS, except it is looking for the average of the values that meet the specified criteria.

This uses the AVERAGE function, not the AVERAGEA function, so the values you want to average have to be numbers or dates. If you try to apply it to a range of values that are all TRUE/FALSE or text values, it will return a #DIV/0! error.

If the range has numbers in it as well as TRUE/FALSE and/or text values, it will only average the number results. (Which means be careful that the range of values you use are all actually numbers since it won't look at any numbers stored as text.)

(Also, you can use it with dates, which are technically numbers. It will give you a date that's within the range of the dates that meet your criteria, I'm just not quite sure how you'd interpret the result.)

There is an AVERAGEIF function, but if you master AVERAGEIFS you won't need to use it.

Since at this point I think you have the general gist of how each of these functions work, let's just look at a few examples.

First, using the data table we used for SUMIFS and COUNTIFS, how would you calculate the average amount customers spent per transaction when they bought Whatsits?

This requires looking at Total Cost based on only one criteria, product. The formula is:

=AVERAGEIFS(E2:E16,C2:C16,"Whatsit")

What if we wanted that same calculation, but for all three product types? Just like with COUNTIFS, it turns out we can do this with an array:

| I2 | | ⌄ | ⁞ | × ✓ | *fx* | =AVERAGEIFS(E:E,C:C,H2:H4) | |
|---|---|---|---|---|---|---|---|

| | H | I | J |
|---|---|---|---|
| 1 | **Product** | **Average Spent** | |
| 2 | Whatsit | $ 10.80 | |
| 3 | Widget | $ 20.81 | |
| 4 | Whatchamacallit | $ 95.25 | |
| 5 | | | |

In this case I put

$$=AVERAGEIFS(E:E,C:C,H2:H4)$$

into Cell I2, and it populated the values for Cells I2 through I4.

Finally, how would you write a formula to calculate the average amount customers spent per transaction on Whatsits in June? I wrote it like this:

$$=AVERAGEIFS(E2:E16,C2:C16,"Whatsit",A2:A16,">=6/1/2020",A2:A16,"<7/1/20")$$

# The MINIFS Function

**Notation:** MINIFS(min_range, criteria_range1, criteria1, …)

**Excel Definition:** Returns the minimum value among cells specified by a given set of conditions or criteria.

MINIFS gives you the minimum value within a range of cells that meet your chosen criteria. There is not a corresponding MINIF function.

MINIFS uses the same type of criteria that we discussed in detail in the SUMIFS chapter, and it will also return an array of values for you like we showed in the SUMIFS, COUNTIFS, and AVERAGEIFS chapters.

Here is an example of results using both MINIFS and MAXIFS to get minimum and maximum spend per transaction for each customer:

| Customer | Min Spent in One Transaction | Max Spent in One Transaction |
|---|---|---|
| Fromer | $ 14.85 | $ 14.85 |
| Gutierrez | $ 1.35 | $ 20.25 |
| Holsen | $ 13.50 | $ 270.00 |
| Jones | $ 18.00 | $ 123.75 |
| Lee | $ 31.50 | $ 33.75 |
| Morales | $ 20.25 | $ 33.75 |
| Phong | $ 14.85 | $ 101.25 |
| Smith | $ 2.70 | $ 9.00 |

This was built with just two formulas:

=MINIFS(E:E,B:B,H2:H9)

in Cell I2 (the second cell in the second column). And in Cell J2:

=MAXIFS(E:E,B:B,H2:H9)

One new little thing to point out for this chapter: If you get results like I did here using an array (the H2:H9 part of each of those formulas), you can't then sort that table of data by the results.

When I first did this one, I had the customer names in random order based on what Remove Duplicates gave me. After I added my MINIFS formula using an array, I tried to sort it alphabetically. It wouldn't let me.

There are two ways to fix that. One is to paste special-values for that table now that the results are there, and then sort.

The other option, which is what I did, was to move the two cells that have the formulas in them to somewhere else for a moment, sort the customer names in the table, and then bring those two formulas back.

Your other option, of course, is to not use an array in the formula. Just write the formulas in Cells I2 and J2 with a reference to H2 only, and then copy the formulas down.

You can still filter a table using an array result without issues. It seems to just be the Sort option that's affected.

# The MAXIFS Function

**Notation:** MAXIFS(max_range, criteria_range1, criteria1, …)

**Excel Definition:** Returns the maximum value among cells specified by a given set of conditions or criteria.

MAXIFS is our final [Function]IFS function, and it takes the maximum from a range of specified cells based on your criteria. By now you hopefully know how that works. If not, go read the SUMIFS chapter and just think "maximum" instead of "sum" everywhere.

Like MINIFS, it does not have a corresponding single criteria function. (This is because by the time they created the MINIFS and MAXIFS functions they had not gotten around to creating a MINIF or MAXIF function yet, so one was never needed.)

In the MINIFS chapter, you can see an example of MAXIFS applied to the data table we've been working with, and looking at transaction amount for each customer.

In this chapter I wanted to bring it all together with a new example that uses COUNTIFS, AVERAGEIFS, MINIFS, and MAXIFS.

On the next page we have a table of test scores for eighteen students in Professor Jones's class. I want to know if there's any difference between how males and females perform:

I'm using arrays here. That means the formula for MAXIFS in Cell I2 is

$$=\text{MAXIFS}(\$A\$2:\$A\$19,\$B\$2:\$B\$19,\$E\$2:\$E\$3)$$

Note that I used $ signs to fix the references to the data table and to the two values I wanted to evaluate. I did that so I could copy the formula in Cell F2 to Cells G2, H2, and I2, and only have to adjust the function name. (I am very lazy, sometimes to the point of creating more work for myself.)

What did that tell us?

We have 8 men and 10 women in the class. The average class score for men is 79 and for women is 94. The range for men is 70 to 94. The range for women is 89 to 100.

| | A | B | C | D | E | F | G | H | I |
|---|---|---|---|---|---|---|---|---|---|
| 1 | Score | Gender | Professor | | | COUNT | AVERAGE | MIN | MAX |
| 2 | 100 | Female | Jones | | Male | 8 | 79.125 | 70 | 94 |
| 3 | 89 | Male | Jones | | Female | 10 | 94.2 | 89 | 100 |
| 4 | 98 | Female | Jones | | | | | | |
| 5 | 89 | Male | Jones | | | | | | |
| 6 | 70 | Male | Jones | | | | | | |
| 7 | 70 | Male | Jones | | | | | | |
| 8 | 71 | Male | Jones | | | | | | |
| 9 | 90 | Female | Jones | | | | | | |
| 10 | 80 | Male | Jones | | | | | | |
| 11 | 70 | Male | Jones | | | | | | |
| 12 | 89 | Female | Jones | | | | | | |
| 13 | 89 | Female | Jones | | | | | | |
| 14 | 91 | Female | Jones | | | | | | |
| 15 | 97 | Female | Jones | | | | | | |
| 16 | 94 | Male | Jones | | | | | | |
| 17 | 95 | Female | Jones | | | | | | |
| 18 | 100 | Female | Jones | | | | | | |
| 19 | 93 | Female | Jones | | | | | | |
| 20 | | | | | | | | | |

It looks like we have a difference there. Just be careful coming to a conclusion as to why. We don't know if that's the teacher's bias, or maybe this class meets at eight in the morning, and there are four male students who are good friends in the class who really like to party on Thursday nights, and end up missing Friday's quizzes.

# The MEDIAN Function

**Notation:** MEDIAN(number1, [number2],…)

**Excel Definition:** Returns the median, or the number in the middle of the set of given numbers.

Alright, shifting gears a bit, let's talk about the MEDIAN function, which returns the middle number in a range of values. Once more, the notation for the function shows number1, number2, etc., but really the input that you're going to provide will almost always be a cell range. Like:

=MEDIAN(A:A)

=MEDIAN(A1:A26)

=MEDIAN(A2:A26)

All of those would return the middle value in a range of numbers in Cells A2 through A26, because MEDIAN ignores any blank cells or cells with text in them. It just looks at numbers. (But do be careful if there are dates in your cell range, because those are numbers to Excel.)

So, simple enough.

One thing to watch out for with MEDIAN, though, is when you have an even number of results. Because it will *average* the two results closest to the middle.

If you have a binary data set, like the one in the image on the next page, that can give a very misleading result.

In this data set, you either win or lose. You either get 100 or you get 0. But the median result (and the average), would tell you that the middle is around 50. It's not. No one ever gets 50. If this was betting money, that's fine. You're going to land around $50 over time. But what if you can't afford to land on zero? It would be important to know that you will half the time.

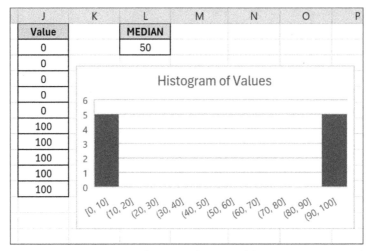

Add one more result on either end, and MEDIAN would return a value of 0 or 100. Which is more honest in a sense? But really MEDIAN is just not the best choice to use for that kind of data.

Graphing your data in some way, like I have here with the histogram, can help you make a better choice about which function to use, if any.

Before we move on, I want to show you an example where MEDIAN is a better choice to use than AVERAGE, and that's in a data set that has "skew" to it, so the "typical" result is not going to be close to the average.

Here we have twenty-five results in Column A that show annual author income:

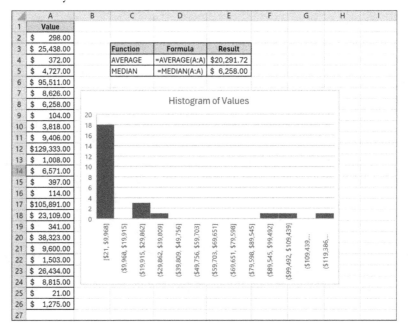

This is made-up data, but it's based on practical experience, too. Most authors don't make much, while some do very, very well. There's also the occasional author who does okay, but not great.

Look at the histogram in the image above. See how most of the values fall in that first bucket? Eighteen out of twenty-five, or 72%, are less than $10,000.

But note, too, that the upper end of this range has someone over $120,000. In this case, $129,333. (In real life, there'd be some over a million.)

In Cell E4 we have the average of the values, $20,291.72. The problem is that because the data has such skew, most authors will never earn that much.

In Cell E5 we have the median of the values, $6,258. That's much more realistic. It's a third of the average, but if you lined up the twenty-five authors and asked the one in the middle what they earned, that's where they'd be. If you were making career decisions off of this data? Much better to have the median than the average.

Now, remember, this is made-up information. Do not actually go out and make life decisions based on it. But if you ever see one of those "the average college grad earns $X" figures, that's a good time to remember that often the highest-earning members of a group skew the average in an unrealistic way. Include just one billionaire in a set of numbers like this, and it looks like everyone is doing well when really only one person is.

Okay. Next up is another way to look at this sort of data, mode.

# The MODE.MULT Function

**Notation:** MODE.MULT(number1, [number2],…)

**Excel Definition:** Returns a vertical array of the most frequently occurring, or repetitive, values in an array or range of data.

This is another one of those functions where the notation lists numbers, but realistically the input you're going to provide is just a single cell range.

What MODE.MULT does is it returns the most common value(s) in your data set. Here:

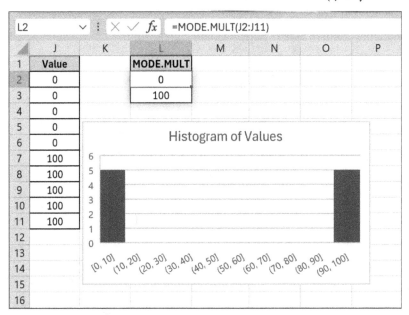

Because 0 and 100 both occur five times, they are both returned when I use MODE.MULT on that range of values. The formula I used is:

$$=MODE.MULT(J2:J11)$$

Very easy.

This is an array function. It will return all of the values that are most-frequently occurring. If there is only one, it will only return one.

Note that it also only works on numbers (including dates, which will return in their numeric form).

If it doesn't have enough room to return all of the values, you'll get a #SPILL! error.

If there are no duplicate values in a range, it will return an #N/A result.

Simple enough.

Two final points to make here.

One, there are two other functions, MODE and MODE.SNGL that are like MODE.MULT but flawed, because they only return one value. So in our example above, where two values occur at equal frequency, they would only return one of them, giving an incomplete result.

Two, MODE.MULT treats each unique value separately. So if you had 98, 99, 100, 1, and 1 in a range, it would return 1 as your most frequent result. Even though 98, 99, and 100 are close to one another, they are each unique values to MODE.MULT. It doesn't group results. So it is often not the best choice if your data isn't in clear distinct buckets like 1 through 5 for customer ratings.

Fortunately, there is another function that you can use to look at how often results fall into various ranges, FREQUENCY. Let's talk about that one now.

# The FREQUENCY Function

**Notation:** FREQUENCY(data_array,bins_array)

**Excel Definition:** Calculates how often values occur within a range of values and then returns a vertical array of numbers having one more element than Bins_array.

The FREQUENCY function is an array function like MODE.MULT, but what it does is lets you count values that fall within a range, not just the most commonly occurring values.

There are two inputs into the FREQUENCY function, your values (the data array) and then the set of values you want to use to create separate buckets to put those numbers into (the bins array).

If you want a count for every single value in your range, then your bins_array input should be the list of unique values (in Column L in the image below):

| M2 | | | fx | =FREQUENCY(J2:J11,L2:L3) | | |
|---|---|---|---|---|---|---|
| | J | K | L | M | N | O |
| 1 | **Value** | | **Unique Values** | **Frequency** | | |
| 2 | 0 | | 0 | 5 | | |
| 3 | 0 | | 100 | 5 | | |
| 4 | 0 | | | 0 | | |
| 5 | 0 | | | | | |
| 6 | 0 | | | | | |
| 7 | 100 | | | | | |
| 8 | 100 | | | | | |
| 9 | 100 | | | | | |
| 10 | 100 | | | | | |
| 11 | 100 | | | | | |
| 12 | | | | | | |

To create that list, copy your values (the same as your data_array input), paste them elsewhere, then apply Remove Duplicates from the Data Tools section of the Data tab to that list. Excel will take the full list of values and reduce it down to one entry for each unique value. You can then use that list as your bins_array.

Once you have your list , put your FREQUENCY formula in the cell next to the first value in the list, like I've done above in Cell M2.

You can see the formula I used:

$$=FREQUENCY(J2:J11,L2:L3)$$

Because my list of values, in this case 0 and 100, is all of the unique values in my data, I end up with a table of each unique value and how often it occurs in my data range.

Note that there is also an "overflow" value in Cell M4 of zero. You need to leave room for that, or else you'll get a #SPILL! error.

Also, I just tested this and it will work even if your list is not in numeric order as long as your list has all of the values in the table.

Now let's look at how to get a count across a *range* of values instead.

It turns out what we did above was not really "count everything equal to 0 or 100". What it actually was, was "count everything up to zero, and then count everything up to 100, and then count everything over 100". It just worked the way it did, because we'd captured all the unique values in the table with the set of bins we used.

But what if you want results that are close to each other to be in the same group, like here:

| | A | B | C | D | E | F | G |
|---|---|---|---|---|---|---|---|
| 1 | Value | | Lower Limit | Upper Limit | Frequency | Percent | |
| 2 | $ 298.00 | | $0 | $500 | 7 | 28% | |
| 3 | $ 25,438.00 | | $501 | $2,500 | 3 | 12% | |
| 4 | $ 372.00 | | $2,501 | $10,000 | 8 | 32% | |
| 5 | $ 4,727.00 | | $10,001 | $50,000 | 4 | 16% | |
| 6 | $ 95,511.00 | | $50,001 | $75,000 | 0 | 0% | |
| 7 | $ 8,626.00 | | $75,001 | $100,000 | 1 | 4% | |
| 8 | $ 6,258.00 | | $100,001 | $125,000 | 1 | 4% | |
| 9 | $ 104.00 | | $125,001 | | 1 | 4% | |
| 10 | $ 3,818.00 | | | | | | |
| 11 | $ 9,406.00 | | | | | | |
| 12 | $129,333.00 | | | | | | |
| 13 | $ 1,008.00 | | | | | | |
| 14 | $ 6,571.00 | | | | | | |
| 15 | $ 397.00 | | | | | | |
| 16 | $ 114.00 | | | | | | |
| 17 | $105,891.00 | | | | | | |
| 18 | $ 23,109.00 | | | | | | |
| 19 | $ 341.00 | | | | | | |
| 20 | $ 38,323.00 | | | | | | |
| 21 | $ 9,600.00 | | | | | | |
| 22 | $ 1,503.00 | | | | | | |
| 23 | $ 26,434.00 | | | | | | |
| 24 | $ 8,815.00 | | | | | | |
| 25 | $ 21.00 | | | | | | |
| 26 | $ 1,275.00 | | | | | | |
| 27 | | | | | | | |

In the table above, I shaded all of the author incomes up to $500 red using conditional formatting. I want those values considered in one group. The way to do that is to use bins_array values that set the upper limit for each bucket.

I did that in Column D. But to make things easier to read, I also put values in Column C that are just there for my or a viewer's information.

Column C is not used by the FREQUENCY function, but putting those values there shows anyone looking at the counts in Column E that we're dealing with a range of values, not one specific value.

For example, the count in E2 is for any author income equal to or less than $500, not just income equal to $500. Without Column C that wouldn't be obvious.

I shaded Column C in gray to visually separate it from the actual input and output of the FREQUENCY function.

Okay.

What is actually driving the FREQUENCY function are the values in Column D. I manually chose those values. They could be anything.

You can see that I did not choose equal intervals. My first one is a $500 range, but the fourth one is a $40,000 range.

I felt like it was important to call out values under $500, but I didn't want a 250-plus row table of results to get to the highest income. So I traded exact comparability between different "buckets" for an easily read table of data.

Whatever values you choose is what Excel will use. It is completely up to you.

The formula here is:

$$=FREQUENCY(A2:A26,D2:D8)$$

Just like with our last example, the results in Column E go one row past the values I gave to Excel. That's because the last bucket is basically a count of anything over the last value you give. In this case, we have one result, $129,333, that gets counted.

Now, counts are all well and good, but I work better with percentages, so I added a calculation in Column F that converts my counts into a percent of the whole calculation. (And shaded it gray since it's not part of the input or the output of the FREQUENCY function.)

With that I can see that 28% of the results are $500 or less and that 32% are between $2,500.01 and $10,000.

If all I wanted was the percentage, I could've combined two functions in Column E to get:

$$=FREQUENCY(A2:A26,D2:D8)/COUNT(A:A)$$

A final note. While FREQUENCY ignores blank cells and text, it does work with dates. Here I have an example looking at how many dates fell in each year range:

| S2 | | | $f_x$ | =FREQUENCY(O2:O11,R2:R5) | | |
|---|---|---|---|---|---|---|
| | O | P | Q | R | S | T |
| 1 | Value | | Beginning | Ending Date | Frequency | |
| 2 | 1/1/2021 | | | 12/31/2019 | 0 | |
| 3 | 1/2/2020 | | 1/1/2020 | 12/31/2020 | 6 | |
| 4 | 3/1/2020 | | 1/1/2021 | 12/31/2021 | 3 | |
| 5 | 3/1/2020 | | 1/1/2022 | 12/31/2022 | 1 | |
| 6 | 1/1/2020 | | 1/1/2023 | | 0 | |
| 7 | 9/2/2021 | | | | | |
| 8 | 3/1/2021 | | | | | |
| 9 | 4/1/2020 | | | | | |
| 10 | 4/1/2020 | | | | | |
| 11 | 3/1/2022 | | | | | |
| 12 | | | | | | |

Cool, huh?

\* \* \*

Alright, I don't know about you, but I've had enough of math for now. Let's move on to a completely different use of Excel functions and look at functions you can use on text.

# The TRIM Function

**Notation:** TRIM(text)

**Excel Definition:** Removes all spaces from a text string except for single spaces between words.

The TRIM function is a good one to know when you need to clean up text entries. Sometimes people will combine text and it will have extra spaces between words, or you'll get data where someone (even yourself) typed an extra space at the end or at the beginning of the entry. TRIM is the way to clean that all up.

It says the input is text, but usually I just reference the cell that contains that text instead.

$$=TRIM(A1)$$

Remember to lock in the result when you're done. I use paste special-values for that. Until you do so, the contents of the new cell are still a formula that references the original cell. If you delete that original cell, you will get a #REF! error in the cell that has your formula.

You can also nest a function within the TRIM function. For example, back in the day I would have used CONCATENATE to join strings of text together into one entry, such as first name, middle name, last name. Problem is, if there's no middle initial, that would generate an extra space in the result. Wrapping TRIM around the function fixed that issue:

$$=TRIM(CONCATENATE(B2," ",C2," ",A2," ",D2))$$

TRIM will also work on numbers that it perceives as text such as 123 456 789.

# The TEXTJOIN Function

**Notation:** TEXTJOIN(delimiter, ignore_empty, text1, …)

**Excel Definition:** Concatenates a list or range of text strings using a delimiter.

TEXTJOIN is a newer function, but it's one I've come to love. (For some reason I can love Excel functions and pets much more easily than humans. Go figure.)

Anyway. What it does is it takes text inputs and joins them into a single entry. You can tell it how to separate those entries with what you provide as the delimiter(s).

You can also tell it how to deal with empty fields so that you don't run into the issue I mentioned with CONCATENATE where you get an extra space and need to use TRIM to clean it up.

Here is our data table and result:

| | A | B | C | D | E | F |
|---|---|---|---|---|---|---|
| 1 | **First Name** | **Middle Initial** | **Last Name** | **Suffix** | **Full Name** | **Formula** |
| 2 | John | | Lee | Jr. | John Lee Jr. | =TEXTJOIN(" ",TRUE,A2:D2) |
| 3 | Sarah | J. | Morales | | Sarah J. Morales | =TEXTJOIN(" ",TRUE,A3:D3) |
| 4 | Lee | K. | Jones | Esq. | Lee K. Jones Esq. | =TEXTJOIN(" ",TRUE,A4:D4) |
| 5 | Ann | | Phong | | Ann Phong | =TEXTJOIN(" ",TRUE,A5:D5) |
| 6 | Jose | A. | Gutierrez | | Jose A. Gutierrez | =TEXTJOIN(" ",TRUE,A6:D6) |
| 7 | Dean | | Holsen | | Dean Holsen | =TEXTJOIN(" ",TRUE,A7:D7) |
| 8 | Francisco | R. | Morales | | Francisco R. Morales | =TEXTJOIN(" ",TRUE,A8:D8) |
| 9 | Marney | B. | Smith | | Marney B. Smith | =TEXTJOIN(" ",TRUE,A9:D9) |
| 10 | Kelly | | Fromer | | Kelly Fromer | =TEXTJOIN(" ",TRUE,A10:D10) |
| 11 | | | | | | |

Columns A through D have the text we want to join together.

Column E is the result of using this TEXTJOIN formula in Row 2 and copying it down:

=TEXTJOIN(" ",TRUE,A2:D2)

Column F shows the formula for each row.

Now let's break that down.

The first input is the delimiter. This is just a fancy way of saying "what is between the entries". The delimiter I used is a single space. I had to put it into quotes since I typed it directly into the function.

The second input is a TRUE/FALSE input where you tell Excel whether to ignore empty cells or not. Since I don't want those weird extra spaces when a middle name or suffix is missing, I put TRUE. If I had said FALSE, there wouldn't be any text to put there, but Excel would include the delimiter, and I'd end up with two spaces next to each other or an extra one at the end.

Finally, the third input is text. Excel lets you list each text reference individually, separated by a comma. But it also let me use a cell range since my inputs were in the order I wanted: A2:D2.

This would also work, it just takes a little more effort to create:

$$=TEXTJOIN(" ",TRUE,A2,B2,C2,D2)$$

If the resulting text string is too long (32,767 characters) Excel will return a #VALUE! error.

TEXTJOIN is very easy to use compared to CONCATENATE or CONCAT, which is how I would've done this before. With those functions, you have to list the delimiter as a separate entry each time, so you have A2," ",B2," ", etc. all the way down the line.

Based on that difference, you might think CONCATENATE (I never used CONCAT but it was the shortened name they came out with at some point) is the way to go if you want to use different delimiters, because you can manually add each one as you create your text string.

But it turns out that TEXTJOIN also lets you have multiple delimiters.

You have two options.

First, you can include them in the function itself by using curly brackets around your list of delimiters, putting each one in quotes, and separating them with a comma. Here, for example, I have space, space, and then a comma with a space:

$$=TEXTJOIN(\{" "," ",", "\},TRUE,A16:D16)$$

It's a little hard to read after the fact, but pretty easy to create.

Second, you can put your delimiters into cells, like I did on the next page in Cells G20 to G22. Cells G20 and G21 have spaces, Cell G22 has a comma and a space.

If you do that, you can then reference that cell range as your first input. For example, the formula I used in Cell G16 was:

$$=TEXTJOIN(\$G\$20:\$G\$22,TRUE,A16:D16)$$

Note that I put $ signs on the cell references for the first input. That lets me copy the formula to other cells while still referencing the range of cells with my delimiters in them.

| | A | B | C | D | G | H |
|---|---|---|---|---|---|---|
| 15 | First Name | Middle Initial | Last Name | Suffix | Full Name | Formula |
| 16 | John | | Lee | Jr. | John Lee Jr. | =TEXTJOIN($G$20:$G$22,TRUE,A16:D16) |
| 17 | Lee | K. | Jones | Esq. | Lee K. Jones, Esq. | =TEXTJOIN($G$20:$G$22,TRUE,A17:D17) |
| 18 | | | | | | |
| 19 | | | | | Delimiters | Description |
| 20 | | | | | | Space |
| 21 | | | | | | Space |
| 22 | | | | | , | Comma, Space |
| 23 | | | | | | |

Now. We have a problem. Look at the values in Cells G16 and G17. G17 is great and perfect and wonderful. Lee K. Jones, Esq. is exactly what we wanted. But John Lee Jr. is not. Why?

Because it turns out that if you give Excel more than one delimiter to use, it will go to that list of delimiters only when it needs one. So what happened here for John Lee Jr. is that it needed a delimiter between John and Lee, so grabbed that first space. Then I told it to skip the middle initial if it was empty, so it did. When it needed another delimiter to put between Lee and Jr., it grabbed the next delimiter in the list, which was the second one, a space.

You might think that the way to solve this is to change that TRUE to a FALSE and surround the whole thing with TRIM. But no. That doesn't work. You end up with a comma at the end of all of the entries that don't have a suffix. (How do I know? I tried it. It's always good to experiment in Excel and see what you get.)

As of now, I think the best way to solve this would be an IFS function (which we discuss later in the book) where you'd use a conditional statement that said "(a) if there's no suffix, then use a space and skip blanks, (b) but if there is a suffix, then don't skip anything and use this list of delimiters but trim out extra spaces".

$$=IFS(ISBLANK(D3),TEXTJOIN("$$
$$",TRUE,A3:D3),TRUE,TRIM(TEXTJOIN(\$G\$20:\$G\$22,FALSE,A3:D3)))$$

It looks ugly, and uses ISBLANK, which is another function we haven't covered that just asks if a cell is blank or not, but I think it works.

Break that down and we have these two TEXTJOIN functions:

$$TEXTJOIN(" ",TRUE,A3:D3)$$

$$TRIM(TEXTJOIN(\$G\$20:\$G\$22,FALSE,A3:D3))$$

Since we used TRUE in the first one, we don't need TRIM. But since we used FALSE for the second one, any time there is a missing middle initial we'd have a double space without TRIM, so we need it.

(That was fun for me, but probably not for you. Just let it sit there for now as one of those things Excel can do if you are willing to explore and experiment to find a solution.)

Okay.

One more thing to know about delimiters. If you use a list of different delimiters, and Excel needs more than the list you gave it, Excel will circle back to the start of your list. So be sure you've thought through the different iterations of your results and how those will work with the delimiters you've provided if you're going to provide more than one delimiter.

# The LEFT Function

**Notation:** LEFT(text, [num_chars])

**Excel Definition:** Returns the specified number of characters from the start of a text string.

The LEFT function is one of three functions you can use to extract part of a text entry. It does exactly what it says it will do. It takes x number of characters from the left of an entry.

Even though it lists the first input as text, I almost always use a cell reference for that first input to indicate where my text is located.

I recently used this on a database of case numbers where some entries were just a number 1234 stored as text, but others were 1234N or 1234Jones. Easy enough for me to extract the number portion from a range of values in Column A with:

$$=LEFT(A2,4)$$

and copy it down all the rows of data.

Of course, that doesn't always work so nicely. Here you can see an example where it didn't work in Row 6:

| | A | B | C |
|---|---|---|---|
| 1 | **Case Number** | **LEFT Result** | **Formula** |
| 2 | 1234 | 1234 | =LEFT(A2,4) |
| 3 | 1234N | 1234 | =LEFT(A3,4) |
| 4 | 1234Jones | 1234 | =LEFT(A4,4) |
| 5 | 123 | 123 | =LEFT(A5,4) |
| 6 | 123N | 123N | =LEFT(A6,4) |
| 7 | | | |

That's because the first four characters in Cell A6 were a three-digit case number followed by an N. It worked okay with Row 5, though, that had just three characters, all the number portion of a case number.

So you have to still pay attention to your data and check your results when you use this.

This was a very clean example for using LEFT. Sometimes I have to get fancier and combine it with other functions, like LEN, if the number of characters needed varies.

Another thing to note, the number of characters input is optional. If you leave it out, you'll get the left-most character in the cell.

There is a counterpart to LEFT, LEFTB, that is designed to work with languages like Chinese, Japanese, and Korean where you specify the number of bytes instead of the number of characters.

# The RIGHT Function

**Notation:** RIGHT(text, [num_chars])

**Excel Definition:** Returns the specified number of characters from the end of a text string.

The RIGHT function works just like the LEFT function, except it pulls the designated characters from the right end of the referenced text.

So, for example, one of the reports I receive sometimes at work is a report that includes entries like 125 USD, 272 AUD, 456 CAD, etc. I use the RIGHT function to extract the currency (USD, AUD, and CAD) from those cells.

=RIGHT(A2,3)

(I can then use LEN and LEFT to pull the numbers as well.)

If you omit the number of characters input, you'll get just the right-most character.

The counterpart to RIGHT for entries in languages like Chinese, Korean, and Japanese is RIGHTB.

# The MID Function

**Notation:** MID(text, start_num, num_chars)

**Excel Definition:** Returns the characters from the middle of a text string, given a starting position and length.

The MID function completes our trio of functions for extracting text from a text string. It's basically for when the text you want isn't on the left or the right end of the text entry, but is somewhere in the middle. Note that it requires an additional input, start_num, because you have to tell it where to start in addition to the number of characters you want.

The inputs to this function are all required, none are optional. If you omit one, Excel will tell you that you didn't provide enough inputs.

Also, you have to provide a value of 1 or more for start_num. You can leave num_chars blank, but then your result will also be blank.

MID also has a counterpart, MIDB, for languages like Chinese, Japanese, and Korean.

Here is a use of MID on the text "$10 dollars" where I want the dollar value:

$$=MID("\$10\ dollars",2,2)$$

The first input is the text, which I provided within the function this time so put in quotes. (It could also be a cell reference like I used with LEFT and RIGHT.)

The second input tells Excel where to start in that text string. Just count characters (including spaces) to where the first character you want is. In this case, I wanted to skip that initial dollar sign and pull the 1, so I wanted to start on the second character.

The third input is how much of the remainder of the text string you want. Here I knew the number I wanted was two digits, so the value I gave Excel was 2.

You will find that for large sets of data that have some variability in them, MID works best when combined with LEN, which we'll discuss next. For example, if the next entry was $123 dollars and the one after that was $1234, this formula wouldn't work.

# The LEN Function

**Notation:** LEN(text)

**Excel Definition:** Returns the number of characters in a text string.

I think of the LEN function as the length function, because that's basically what it's doing. It's telling you the length of a text string. It only has one input, the text you want Excel to use to count the number of characters. As with RIGHT, LEFT, and MID, that first input can be a cell reference. LEN also has a LENB counterpart.

Let's revisit that example from the MID chapter. It was easy enough for me to extract the number from $10 dollars using MID. But then that wasn't going to work for $123 dollars or $1234 dollars.

But let's look at those again:

$10 dollars

$123 dollars

$1234 dollars

They're pretty consistent, aren't they? They all start with a currency symbol ($), then there's the number that can vary in length, then there's a space, and then the word "dollars".

We could manually count the number of characters in " dollars" (8), or we could use

=LEN(" dollars")

to have Excel count for us.

But we still need one more piece of information to extract the number. We need the length of the entire text string. Fortunately, LEN can calculate that, too.

Perfect. Now let's look at some sample data and apply it:

| | A | B | C | D |
|---|---|---|---|---|
| 1 | Value | Number Only | Easy Formula | Hard Formula |
| 2 | $10 dollars | 10 | =MID(A2,2,LEN(A2)-9) | =MID(A2,2,LEN(A2)-(LEN(" dollars")+1)) |
| 3 | $123 dollars | 123 | =MID(A3,2,LEN(A3)-9) | =MID(A3,2,LEN(A3)-(LEN(" dollars")+1)) |
| 4 | $1234 dollars | 1234 | =MID(A4,2,LEN(A4)-9) | =MID(A4,2,LEN(A4)-(LEN(" dollars")+1)) |
| 5 | | | | |

Column A has the value we want to extract from, Column B has the result, and Columns C and D have different formulas for how to do this.

Column C has the more manual version, which for Row 2 is:

$$=MID(A2,2,LEN(A2)-9)$$

Let's break that down. It says, "Look in Cell A2, go to the second character, and pull x characters where x is equal to the length of the entire entry minus 9." Why 9? Because we need to remove the dollar sign, the space, and the word dollars to get to the length of the actual number we're trying to extract.

Column D has a version where I have Excel do the math on how many characters to exclude:

$$=MID(A2,2,LEN(A2)-(LEN(" dollars")+1))$$

Instead of my putting in the value 9, I have:

$$(LEN(" dollars")+1)$$

Okay. So hopefully you can now see how to use RIGHT, LEFT, MID, and LEN to extract part of a text entry. Now let's cover two new functions that may make this even easier, TEXTBEFORE and TEXTAFTER.

# The TEXTBEFORE Function

**Notation:** TEXTBEFORE(text, delimiter, [instance_num], [match_mode], [match_end], [if_not_found])

**Excel Definition:** Returns text that's before delimiting characters.

They make this look really complicated, don't they? But really it's just a big fancy function to say "I want the text that falls before this other text."

Note that the only required inputs are the text and the delimiter. All the rest is optional.

So let's go back to Cell A2 with its entry of "$10 dollars" from the last chapter.

If I want to extract the dollar sign and number, so drop the part that says " dollars", I can just write:

=TEXTBEFORE(A2," dollars")

For me personally, it's easier to understand what I'm telling it to do to use " dollars", but that doesn't mean I can't simplify it down later. I could actually use:

=TEXTBEFORE(A2," ")

That tells Excel to pull everything before the first space. Since there is only one space in the entry, it's that simple.

Okay. So that is TEXTBEFORE at its most basic. Your first input is the text or cell reference where the text is. Your second input is where in that text to draw the line.

But you can get fancier.

The third input is instance_num. Sometimes you'll have a text string and want to remove the text before a certain point, but maybe the delimiter you want to use for that is one that appears earlier in that text string, too.

Here is an example:

| | A | B | C |
|---|---|---|---|
| 8 | **Value** | **Isolate Name** | **Formula** |
| 9 | John Lee Investigator | John Lee | =TEXTBEFORE(A9," ",2) |
| 10 | Lee Jones Lawyer | Lee Jones | =TEXTBEFORE(A10," ",2) |
| 11 | Kelly Fromer Teacher | Kelly Fromer | =TEXTBEFORE(A11," ",2) |
| 12 | | | |

I have three listings where the information is first name, space, last name, space, profession. To isolate just the name in Cell A9, I can use:

$$=TEXTBEFORE(A9," ",2)$$

That's saying, "Look at the text in Cell A9, find the second space, and bring back everything before that point".

If the text entries had been something like "Kelly Fromer, Teacher" then we'd need to use a comma and a space as our delimiter:

$$=TEXTBEFORE(A13,", ")$$

Of course, as you may remember when we were using TEXTJOIN, data isn't always that neat and tidy. You may have variation in the number of spaces in different cells.

It turns out, your instance number can also be a negative number.

If you do that, Excel will start at the end instead of the beginning of your text. So with entries like, "Joseph L. Jones, Jr., Teacher" and "Daphne Clark, Astronaut" I'd use:

$$=TEXTBEFORE(A21,",",-1)$$

That looks for a comma delimiter, but it does it from the end, so I don't end up dropping the suffix from someone's name. (I don't need to include the space after the comma in the delimiter, because we're pulling everything to the left of the comma. I could use it, but it's not needed.)

The match_mode input lets you say whether Excel should be case-sensitive when it looks for the delimiter.

This was another one that I had a hard time thinking up an example for, but with my Google book links, I'll often add &gl= and then the two letter country abbreviation at the end to link to Google stores in different countries. So let's say I was trying to extract a website address that didn't have that on the end. TEXTBEFORE is one way I could do that.

Here we go:

| | A | B | C |
|---|---|---|---|
| 13 | **Website*** | **Case-Sensitive** | **Formula** |
| 14 | www.Abs&Glutes.com&gl=AU | www.Abs&Glutes.com | =TEXTBEFORE(A14,"&gl",,0) |
| 15 | | **Not Case-Sensitive** | **Formula** |
| 16 | | www.Abs | =TEXTBEFORE(A14,"&gl",,1) |
| 17 | | | |
| 18 | *Completely made up - do not blame me if it's real and weird. | | |
| 19 | | | |

This (made up) website address, Abs&Glutes.com, includes &Gl in the name. If I don't tell Excel to treat my delimiter, &gl, as case-sensitive, Excel won't pull the full website address for me.

The formula I need is:

$$=TEXTBEFORE(A14,"\&gl",,0)$$

where that 0 in the last position tells Excel to treat &gl separate from &Gl.

Another thing to note about the formula I used here is that I didn't need the instance_num input, so I just left it blank. If you're not comfortable doing that, you could also use:

$$=TEXTBEFORE(A14,"\&gl",1,0)$$

The next optional input is match_end, which according to Excel "treats the end of text as a delimiter". I went to the help text to understand what this meant, but it was not in fact helpful.

I think I know what this is for, though. If you use a delimiter that isn't contained in the text in that cell—so a comma when the cell has no commas—Excel is going to by default generate a #N/A error as your result. But if you put 1 for this input, Excel will instead return the full text in the cell.

If you want something else returned instead of the full text or #N/A, that's where the final input, if_not_found, can be used. It only gets used if the input before it for match_end is 0 or blank, *and* there is no match to the delimiter.

You can use a number for this input. Excel will return that number as text. If you want to put actual text, be sure to surround the text with quote marks.

Here is an example with text:

$$=TEXTBEFORE(A23,",",,0,0,"Nothing There")$$

I suspect you'll only use the last two optional inputs when you're getting some sort of error in your results that needs to be overcome by suppressing the #N/A error, which can interfere in certain calculations.

The other time you may see a #N/A error for this function is if the instance_num you use is greater than the number of times the delimiter occurs in the text.

You may also see a #VALUE! error if the instance_num you use is a larger number than the length of the text in the cell. So, for example, 4 in a cell that only has the word "ten".

You will also see that if you list zero for the instance_num.

Okay, that was kind of fun to explore, let's now look at its counterpart, TEXTAFTER.

# The TEXTAFTER Function

**Notation:** TEXTAFTER(text, delimiter, [instance_num], [match_mode], [match_end], [if_not_found])

**Excel Definition:** Returns the text that's after delimiting characters.

TEXTAFTER is the counterpart to TEXTBEFORE. They actually have the exact same inputs, it's just which side of the delimiter you return.

Let's revisit two of our examples from the TEXTBEFORE chapter:

| | A | B | C |
|---|---|---|---|
| 8 | Value | Isolate Profession | Formula |
| 9 | John Lee Investigator | Investigator | =TEXTAFTER(A9," ",2) |
| 10 | Lee Jones Lawyer | Lawyer | =TEXTAFTER(A10," ",2) |
| 11 | Kelly Fromer Teacher | Teacher | =TEXTAFTER(A11," ",2) |
| 12 | | | |
| 13 | Value | Isolate Profession | Formula |
| 14 | Joseph L. Jones, Jr., Teacher | Teacher | =TEXTAFTER(A14,", ",-1) |
| 15 | Daphne Clark, Astronaut | Astronaut | =TEXTAFTER(A15,", ",-1) |
| 16 | | | |

In Rows 9 through 11 I had first name, last name, profession, all separated by a single space. To get the profession from those cells, all I had to do was change my TEXTBEFORE formula that extracted the names to TEXTAFTER:

$$=TEXTAFTER(A9," ",2)$$

This formula looks in Cell A9, finds the second space, and brings back everything after that.

In Rows 14 and 15 we have profession separated out with a comma and a space, but there's also a name with a comma and a space before the suffix.

Fortunately, I can use a delimiter that is a comma and space combined, and then a -1 for instance_num to pull profession:

$$=TEXTAFTER(A14,", ",-1)$$

Just like with TEXTBEFORE, the match_mode input is used to determine if the delimiter should be case-sensitive. Match_end is used to return the entire cell contents instead of an #N/A result when there's no match to the delimiter, and if_not_found is used to return a custom result instead of #N/A or the entire cell contents.

One final example for you.

In the MID chapter, we wanted to extract just the number from entries like $123 dollars and $1234 dollars. You can also do that using a combination of TEXTBEFORE and TEXTAFTER. Specifically:

$$=TEXTBEFORE(TEXTAFTER(A2,"\$")," ")$$

That says, "take text after the dollar sign and then, from that result, take the text from before the first space".

It might be easier to understand written as:

$$=TEXTBEFORE(TEXTAFTER(A2,"\$")," dollars")$$

But that limits it to entries that use dollars, whereas the first example would work with a variety of currencies.

Also, for the bored overachievers, it turns out you can give Excel a list of delimiters to use with these ones, too.

Here I have a variety of currency entries, and I want to remove the currency symbol from before all of them. I can do that with a TEXTAFTER formula:

| | A | B | C |
|---|---|---|---|
| 17 | Value | Remove Currency Symbol | Formula |
| 18 | $10 dollars | 10 dollars | =TEXTAFTER(A18,{"$","£","€"}) |
| 19 | £123 pounds | 123 pounds | =TEXTAFTER(A19,{"$","£","€"}) |
| 20 | €1234 euros | 1234 euros | =TEXTAFTER(A20,{"$","£","€"}) |
| 21 | €1234 euros, $10 dollars, £123 pounds | 1234 euros, $10 dollars, £123 pounds | =TEXTAFTER(A21,{"$","£","€"}) |
| 22 | $10 dollars, £123 pounds, €1234 euros | 10 dollars, £123 pounds, €1234 euros | =TEXTAFTER(A22,{"$","£","€"}) |

Look at Rows 18 to 20. What I did here is used curly brackets around the different delimiters I wanted Excel to use.

$$=TEXTAFTER(A18,{"\$","£","€"})$$

It looked for each delimiter and then when it found one of them, extracted the text past that point. Pretty cool, huh?

But now look at Rows 21 and 22 where it didn't work so well. Note that it stopped as soon as there was a match to any delimiter, so you can't extract all of the currency symbols this way.

Based on the results in those rows, I think Excel starts at the first character and goes through its list looking for each delimiter you give it. If there's a hit on a delimiter, it will give you all the text after that point. If not, it goes to the next *character* in the text, and does the same thing. Not very helpful for a scenario like in Rows 21 and 22, but very nice for Rows 18 and 20, especially if you referenced a cell range for your delimiters. Like this:

=TEXTAFTER(A28,$D$28:$D$30)

where the delimiter values are in Cells D28 to D30 instead of listed directly in the function.

If I had a really long list of data entries I was working with, that included a variety of currency symbols, I'd probably use LEFT to extract them from all my entries, and then Remove Duplicates to create a unique list of the currency symbols in my data, that I could then reference with my TEXTAFTER formula.

(Of course, then we have to pause and ask why we're doing that, because if you are going to add those numbers together, that would be a very bad idea. You'd still need them to be separated by currency type because you can't just add USD, BRL, JPY, etc. values to one another without converting everything to one currency. Right? Right.)

Okay, enough nerding out on that. On to the next. Three more text-related functions to cover, and then we'll get to some date functions. Are you excited? No? Fair enough.

# The LOWER Function

**Notation:** LOWER(text)

**Excel Definition:** Converts all letters in a text string to lowercase.

You are less likely to need this function in Excel than the equivalent option in Word, but it (and its related functions that we'll cover in a moment) is still useful to know.

What LOWER does is it takes a text string and puts all of the text in lower case. While you could enter the text directly into the function itself by using quotes

$$=LOWER("ALRIGHT")$$

you are more likely to use a cell reference with this function.

So why use it? It can help sometimes to convert different entries like "ALRIGHT", "Alright" and "alright" to the same case.

Whether lower case is the best choice is another question, but standardizing capitalization is probably where I would use this the most.

Keep in mind that this is still a function, so until you paste special-values or otherwise lock in the result(s) as text, it is still a formula that is referencing the initial cell. If you delete that initial cell, your formula result will turn into a #REF! error.

# The UPPER Function

**Notation:** UPPER(text)

**Excel Definition:** Converts a text string to all uppercase letters.

The UPPER function is like the LOWER function except it puts everything in upper case letters.

It works the same way. You can enter text directly into the function using quote marks around the text, or reference a cell that contains your text.

And the same caution as with LOWER. This is a formula. Lock it in before moving on so that you don't end up with an error message if you delete the source cell(s). There is an example using UPPER in the next chapter.

# The PROPER Function

**Notation:** PROPER(text)

**Excel Definition:** Converts a text string to proper case; the first letter in each word to uppercase, and all other letters to lowercase.

The PROPER function is the final in this trio of functions. What it does is capitalizes every single word.

This is not the same as title case, which has a set of rules about which words to capitalize. For example, in title case you generally don't capitalize "to" or "and" in a title. Proper just goes through and capitalizes each and every first letter of a word. (Excel does not have a title case option.)

Same caveats. You can reference text directly using quotes, but are more likely to reference a cell that contains your text, and you should lock down the result after you're done.

All three of these are good functions to wrap around another function. So, for example, you may use TEXTJOIN to bring together the text in three different cells. Wrapping that text in LOWER, UPPER, or PROPER would then create standardized capitalization for your finalized entries.

For example, on the next page is a screenshot of different ways I used UPPER and PROPER to create a standardized address entry.

In Row 2 there are values for the street (123 man St in Cell F2), city (El paso in Cell G2), and state (Tx in Cell H2), but they're not capitalized properly.

In Row 5 I used TEXTJOIN to create an address entry. Within that, I used PROPER to capitalize the street and city names, and UPPER to capitalize the state abbreviation:

=TEXTJOIN(", ",TRUE,PROPER(F2),PROPER(G2),UPPER(H2))

The result was:

123 Main St, El Paso, TX

| | E | F | G | H |
|---|---|---|---|---|
| 1 | | **Text 1** | **Text 2** | **Text 3** |
| 2 | | 123 main St | El paso | Tx |
| 3 | | | | |
| 4 | **Formula** | =TEXTJOIN(", ",TRUE,PROPER(F2),PROPER(G2),UPPER(H2)) | | |
| 5 | **Result** | 123 Main St, El Paso, TX | | |
| 6 | | | | |
| 7 | **Formula** | =TEXTJOIN(", ",TRUE,UPPER(F2:H2)) | | |
| 8 | **Result** | 123 MAIN ST, EL PASO, TX | | |
| 9 | | | | |
| 10 | **Formula** | =UPPER(TEXTJOIN(", ",TRUE,F2:H2)) | | |
| 11 | **Result** | 123 MAIN ST, EL PASO, TX | | |
| 12 | | | | |

Much better. I took a different approach in Row 8, and put everything into upper case within the TEXTJOIN function:

$$=TEXTJOIN(", ",TRUE,UPPER(F2:H2))$$

That gave me:

123 MAIN ST, EL PASO, TX

In Row 11, I created the same result by wrapping UPPER around the TEXTJOIN function instead using:

$$=UPPER(TEXTJOIN(", ",TRUE,F2:H2))$$

Since it's only one function being applied to all of the text entries, UPPER can go on the outside of TEXTJOIN just as easily as on the inside.

Okay, enough of text, on to dates.

# Excel and Dates

Before we explore various functions related to dates in Excel, it's important to review how Excel handles dates. What I'm going to discuss here applies to PCs. If you have a Mac, the start date is different.

Behind the scenes, each date is stored as a number. If you type the number 1 into a cell in Excel, and then convert that to a date, you will see that Excel views the number 1 and the date 1/1/1900 as equivalent. Each date from that point forward moves forward by one whole number.

If you are ever dealing with specific times in Excel, it treats hours, minutes, and seconds as fractions of a number. So the value 3.25 is also the date and time January 3, 1900 at 6:00 AM. You have twenty-four hours in a day, and 6:00 AM is one-fourth of the way through a day. The number 3 is two days past the start date of January 1, 1900.

This is nice, because it's lets you easily do math with dates. You can quickly calculate the number of days between two dates using subtraction, because to Excel that's just like subtracting 42321 from 42444.

But you have to be careful with dates in Excel, too.

First, Excel can't handle dates before January 1, 1900. It doesn't convert those to numbers, they are seen as text and not seen as dates. I personally have worked with at least one data set (that included founding dates for companies that dated back to the 1800s) where this became a problem. I ended up with a data set where Excel could not work with some of the values.

The other thing you need to know about dates in Excel is that if you give Excel just part of a date, it will guess the rest of the date. So if I put in Jan-2025, Excel is going to turn that into January 25 of the current year and give it a numeric value. January-2025 becomes January 1, 2025. If you put 3/4 and tab to another cell, Excel will convert that to a month and day of the current year; for me, March 4, 2025.

You won't automatically see this in what displays in the cell, though.

If you go back and click on that cell, you can see the full date in the formula bar.

Excel will always create a full date. Always.

This becomes especially important if you, like me, are a little lazy, and only put the last two years for your dates.

Excel has a rule for how it assigns each two-digit year to a century. As I write this it is the mid- 2020s, and Excel is going to look at an entry like 1/1/35 and turn it into 1935 even though I am more likely to mean 2035.

According to the Excel website help, as of right now, a two-digit year ending in 00 through 29 is interpreted as the years 2000 through 2029, but a two-digit year ending in 30 through 99 is interpreted as the years 1930 through 1999.

We are about three years from that being a big issue with new data inputs.

You can manually change the setting in your systems to modify which years end up in which centuries, but I think the better bet is to really try hard to always use a four-digit year, because if it's computer-dependent, it's way too easy to forget that a different computer doesn't work the way yours does.

To learn more about this, look for a help topic on how two-digit years are interpreted.

In the past I've thought this was a big issue for older data, too, but I've finally realized it's not.

Because Excel converts every date to a number when you enter it, that century assignment by Excel locks in at the time you enter your date.

Which means whatever conversion issue exists only exists at that point in time. Enter the date correctly and you're fine.

So this is something you should pay close attention to when you or other users enter your data. If you know you have a system where all dates need to be in the future, maybe set up a rule to restrict what can be entered into those cells. Or apply conditional formatting to flag entries that are in the past.

One final comment on dates. If you're ever subtracting dates and getting weird results, it may be worth checking to see if the dates you're using include time of day information.

Usually when I'm dealing with dates, I want them to be whole numbers. I want today, but not today at two in the afternoon.

To fix dates that include time information, TRUNC will cut off a number to make it a whole number. Which means using something like:

$$=TRUNC(G21,0)-TRUNC(G22,0)$$

where your dates are in Cells G21 and G22, will ensure that you don't get a wonky answer based on time of day information that changes the result. (Say, 11:45 PM on Monday subtracted from 2:00 AM on Tuesday giving a zero answer instead of 1.)

Okay. Now let's discuss some actual date-related functions.

# The TODAY Function

**Notation:** TODAY()

**Excel Definition:** Returns the current date formatted as a date.

The TODAY function does exactly what it says, it returns the current date. Behind the scenes the value is a whole number. So it's today's date at midnight.

Note that there is no required input into the TODAY function, so you just use opening and closing parens with nothing between them when you use it, whether it gets used standalone or as part of a larger formula.

It's a great one to know about in case you ever have calculations where you want to know the number of days from now. So, maybe you want to know which bills are over 30 days past due. You can use the date of the invoice and TODAY to make that calculation. Here is what that formula looks like where the date of the invoice is in Cell A2:

$$=TODAY()-A2$$

I would probably pair this with an IF or IFS function to suppress any results for customers who still have time to pay before being overdue. Like this:

$$=IF(TODAY()-A2<30,"",TODAY()-A2)$$

What that formula basically says is that if taking today's date and subtracting the date in cell A2 gives you a value less than 30, then just return a blank result, otherwise do the calculation. (We're going to cover IF and IFS soon, so flag this as something to come back to then.)

If you don't lock in your result, each time you open that file, TODAY will pull the current date. Depending on what you're using it for, you may not want that, so be sure to lock the result down immediately if needed.

(This happens often in Word. People will use the equivalent of the TODAY function to create a memo template, and then use the template but fail to lock in the date field when they use it. Six months later they go to open that important memo showing that they did X on Y date and the memo shows the current day's date instead. Yikes. Not something you want to have happen.)

If the time of day is also important, then you need to use a different function, NOW. Let's discuss that one next.

# The NOW Function

**Notation:** NOW()

**Excel Definition:** Returns the current date and time formatted as a date and time.

NOW is very much like TODAY except it will also return the time of day down to the second.

Behind the scenes, instead of getting a whole number, you will get a number that includes a decimal portion representing the current hour, minute, and second.

You can't see on the surface that it goes to the second, but if you use

$$=SECOND(A2)$$

where A2 is the cell that contains your NOW result, you can then use F9 to refresh the result and see it change. (Or you can just trust me on this.)

Like TODAY, NOW has no inputs, just include the opening and closing parens so that Excel can recognize it as a function and not a named value.

To write it standalone:

$$=NOW()$$

To use it in a formula:

$$=NOW()-A2$$

or

$$=A2-NOW()$$

Don't forget, that if you need to lock your result down immediately, you can either use paste special-values or type your formula in like normal but then use F9 to convert it from a formula to a calculation. If you use F9 it will return the numerical equivalent of the date, so you'll need to reformat the result.

# The YEAR Function

**Notation:** YEAR(serial_number)

**Excel Definition:** Returns the year of a date, an integer in the range 1900-9999.

The YEAR function lets you extract the year portion of a date. (In the function notation date is referred to as a serial number.)

So if I have 1/15/2024 as my date in Cell A2, then:

$$=YEAR(A2)$$

will return a result of 2024.

# The MONTH Function

**Notation:** MONTH(serial_number)

**Excel Definition:** Returns the month, a number from 1 (January) to 12 (December).

The MONTH function works just like the YEAR function except the value it returns is a number between 1 and 12 that represents which month that date falls in.

Again, Excel stores dates behind the scenes as numbers, so it doesn't matter to Excel whether you write dates like an American with 7/1/24 meaning July 1, 2024 or like a European where that is January 7, 2024.

Theoretically, your version of Excel is set to your geographic location so it stored that date properly for you when you entered it.

But if you are having weird calculation issues around dates, then maybe that's something worth checking by using the MONTH function. Point it at that 7/1/24 entry and see what it returns for you.

So, for a date in Cell A1 you'd use:

=MONTH(A1)

# The DAY Function

**Notation:** DAY(serial_number)

**Excel Definition:** Returns the day of the month, a number from 1 to 31.

The DAY function is like the MONTH function except it will return the number for the day portion of a date. July 1, 2024 will give a result of 1.

$$=DAY(A1)$$

where A1 contains your date. Or

$$=DAY("1/12/25")$$

$$=DAY(45669)$$

if you want to use the date in the formula.

Again, since Excel stores dates as numbers, the order in which someone might write a date when they enter it shouldn't impact the result as long as they provide the date in the correct format for their location.

As you can probably guess at this point, there are also functions for HOUR, MINUTE, and SECOND. They work the exact same way. If you have a whole number, like I did above, they will return a result of zero, so they really only provide useful information when you have time of day included in a date.

# The TEXT Function

**Notation:** TEXT(value, format_text)

**Excel Definition:** Converts a value to text in a specific number format.

There is one aspect of the TEXT function that I love and the rest of it I think you should never try to learn. In the past I've covered both to be thorough, but I'm not going to do that this time. You can look it up if you want.

Okay. So what TEXT does that I love, is it can take a date and return the name for the month or the day of the week. Here are examples using March 7, 2024:

| | A | B | C |
|---|---|---|---|
| 1 | **Date** | **Formula** | **Result** |
| 2 | 3/7/2024 | =TEXT(A2,"d") | 7 |
| 3 | 3/7/2024 | =TEXT(A3,"dd") | 07 |
| 4 | 3/7/2024 | =TEXT(A4,"ddd") | Thu |
| 5 | 3/7/2024 | =TEXT(A5,"dddd") | Thursday |
| 6 | 3/7/2024 | =TEXT(A6,"m") | 3 |
| 7 | 3/7/2024 | =TEXT(A7,"mm") | 03 |
| 8 | 3/7/2024 | =TEXT(A8,"mmm") | Mar |
| 9 | 3/7/2024 | =TEXT(A9,"mmmm") | March |
| 10 | 3/7/2024 | =TEXT(A10,"y") | 24 |
| 11 | 3/7/2024 | =TEXT(A11,"yyy") | 2024 |
| 12 | | | |

Column A has the date. Column B has the formula I used for each row. Column C has the result of that formula.

The first four rows have formulas for returning the day portion of the date.

$$=TEXT(A2,"d")$$

$$=TEXT(A3,"dd")$$

=TEXT(A4,"ddd")

=TEXT(A5,"dddd")

A single d in quotes will return the one-digit day value, 7, two will return a two-digit result, 07, three will return the short name of the day of the week, Thu, and four returns the long name of the day of the week, Thursday.

The next four rows do the same for month using "m", "mm", "mmm", or "mmmm". And you get similar results. A one-digit month, a two-digit month, the abbreviated month name, the full month name.

The final two rows use "y" or "yyy" to return a two-digit year or a four-digit year. (You could also use "yy" or "yyyy" to return a two-digit and four-digit year, respectively.)

If you put the text for the second input into a cell, you can just reference the cell, no need for quotes:

=TEXT(A2,E1)

Converting dates to their name has come in handy for me more than once. The original reason I figured out you could do this was because I needed to know days of the week for a large table of dates, and figured there had to be some way to do it, which, fortunately, there is.

\* \* \*

Okay. On to the next section.

We only have eight functions left, but two of them are two of the most useful ones you'll learn, IFS and XLOOKUP, but also some of the harder ones to use when you're just getting started. (Unless your mind naturally works that way, of course. We are all wired differently.)

# The IF Function

**Notation:** IF(logical_test, [value_if_true], [value_if_false])

**Excel Definition:** Checks whether a condition is met, and returns one value if TRUE, and another value if FALSE.

The IF function will always be one of my first loves even though the IFS function is a much better choice for most uses these days. It still has its uses though, so I want to cover it here first before we move on to IFS.

At its heart, the IF function lets you give two possible answers. Think of writing an IF function as saying, if this is true, then return that result, but if it isn't true, then return another result.

That seems pretty basic, right? Okay, so you can return two different results, who cares? Oh my sweet summer child, there is so much power in being able to react in real-time to different outcomes.

(Especially when you have more than two possible outcomes, but that's what IFS is for.)

I mean, think about real life. If someone is nice to you, you want to be nice to them. But if they hit you, you probably want the choice to react differently, don't you? You don't want to only be able to be nice no matter what.

(Clearly I am writing this chapter at the end of a long week. Let's get it back on track with some examples. But first let's look at the inputs.)

The first input to the IF function is described as "logical_test". This is the question you are asking. Is the value in Cell A2 greater than 5? Does it contain this word? Is the result of that formula TRUE?

The second input, value_if_true, is what to do if the answer to that question is yes.

The third (and final) input, value_if_false, is what to do if the answer to that question is no.

Now, it looks like they're both optional, right? They're both in brackets. But actually, you must have one or the other. You will get an error message if you only have one input for the IF function.

So let's go back to that IF function I shared earlier for TODAY:

$$=IF(TODAY()-A2<0,"",TODAY()-A2)$$

What was the question I was asking? Let's look at what I listed for the first input:

$$TODAY()-A2<0$$

That's asking if today's date minus the date in Cell A2 is less than zero.
If it is, what did I tell Excel to do?

$$""$$

That basically is returning a blank result. I could've also used

$$=IF(TODAY()-A2<0,,TODAY()-A2)$$

but that returns a result of 0 and I'd prefer it to look blank.
I could've just as easily had it return text, and used something like:

$$"NOT DUE YET"$$

Or a value

$$5$$

Or the value in a cell:

$$A2$$

Any of those would work. You can see that text requires quotes, but the others just need to be listed between the commas.

Finally, what did I tell Excel to do if it *wasn't* true? That's the last input to the function:

$$TODAY()-A2$$

I told Excel to go ahead and display the result of the calculation.

This is a very common use of IF for me. I like to suppress messy error messages that are only there because there's no data yet. There are other functions like IFERROR that can also do that for you, that we'll cover soon, but they're so easy to do, I just build my own.

For example. If I use

$$=B1/C1$$

and there's no value in Cell C1, then I get a #DIV/0! error message. I will often do this instead:

$$=IF(C1="","",B1/C1)$$

That's just saying, if Cell C1 is blank, keep this cell blank, too. Otherwise, divide the value in B1 by the value in C1.

Okay.

So that was the basic approach with IF functions. Think of them as IF – THEN – ELSE statements. Those are your three inputs. If you can figure out how to describe your question as a calculation, that's your first input. And then you tell Excel what to do if that's true (THEN) and what to do if it isn't (ELSE).

If you're good with what we've talked about so far and don't want to go further, skip the rest of this chapter. But for the curious, let's keep going.

Before IFS existed, I did a lot more with the IF function using what I refer to as nested IF statements. This may be something you'll see in older Excel files, or that you yourself may need if you ever have to use an older version of Excel.

Think of a nested IF statement as saying, "If this is true then do A, but if it isn't true then is this other thing true? If it is, do B. Otherwise, is this third thing true? If so do C. Otherwise do D."

For our visual learners, this is what that looks like drawn out:

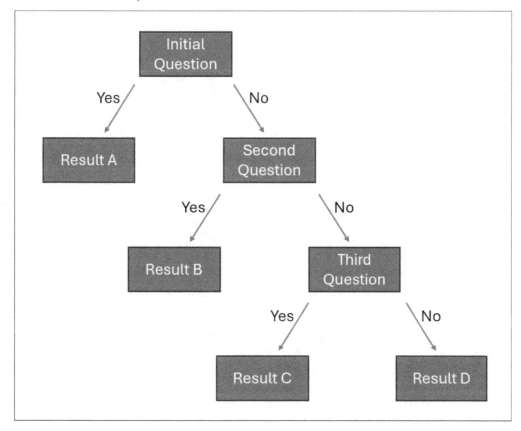

You can keep going as long as you want with that. I've gone nine or ten IF statements deep that way. The only real constraint is the challenge in writing one of these without making a mistake.

The classic example I've used in the past for this was a discount table. I think nowadays I'd use XLOOKUP instead, but the example still holds, so let's use it.

Here we go:

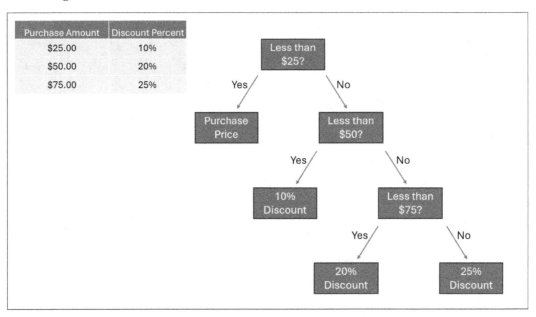

In the top left corner of this image, I have a discount table. If you spend $25, you get a 10% discount. Spend $50, get 20%. Spend $75, get 25%. I've also translated that into our IF-THEN-ELSE flowchart.

First question, is the amount less than $25? If so, you pay the purchase price. No discount.

Next question, is it less than $50? (Implied in the second question is that it is $25 or more already.) If so, then you get a 10% discount.

Final question, is it less than $75? (Implied here is that it is $50 or more.) If so, then you get a 20% discount. If not, then it must be $75 or more and you get a 25% discount.

On the next page is a table of values using that discount table where the price after discount is calculated using nested IF functions.

Our table is in Cells A1 through B4. Row 8 is the first calculation for a purchase price of $25:

=IF($A8<$A$2,$A8,IF($A8<$A$3,$A8*(1-$B$2),IF($A8<$A$4,$A8*(1-$B$3),$A8*(1-$B$4))))

| | A | B | C | D | E |
|---|---|---|---|---|---|
| 1 | **Purchase Amount** | **Discount Percent** | | | |
| 2 | $25.00 | 10% | | | |
| 3 | $50.00 | 20% | | | |
| 4 | $75.00 | 25% | | | |
| 5 | | | | | |
| 6 | | | | | |
| 7 | **Customer Purchases** | **Price after Discount** | | **Formula** | |
| 8 | $25.00 | $22.50 | | =IF($A8<$A$2,$A8,IF($A8<$A$3,$A8*(1-$B$2),IF($A8<$A$4,$A8*(1-$B$3),$A8*(1-$B$4)))) | |
| 9 | $50.00 | $40.00 | | =IF($A9<$A$2,$A9,IF($A9<$A$3,$A9*(1-$B$2),IF($A9<$A$4,A9*(1-$B$3),$A9*(1-$B$4)))) | |
| 10 | $75.00 | $56.25 | | =IF($A10<$A$2,$A10,IF($A10<$A$3,$A10*(1-$B$2),IF($A10<$A$4,A10*(1-$B$3),$A10*(1-$B$4)))) | |
| 11 | $15.00 | $15.00 | | =IF($A11<$A$2,$A11,IF($A11<$A$3,$A11*(1-$B$2),IF($A11<$A$4,A11*(1-$B$3),$A11*(1-$B$4)))) | |
| 12 | $60.00 | $48.00 | | =IF($A12<$A$2,$A12,IF($A12<$A$3,$A12*(1-$B$2),IF($A12<$A$4,A12*(1-$B$3),$A12*(1-$B$4)))) | |
| 13 | $80.00 | $60.00 | | =IF($A13<$A$2,$A13,IF($A13<$A$3,$A13*(1-$B$2),IF($A13<$A$4,A13*(1-$B$3),$A13*(1-$B$4)))) | |
| 14 | $40.00 | $36.00 | | =IF($A14<$A$2,$A14,IF($A14<$A$3,$A14*(1-$B$2),IF($A14<$A$4,A14*(1-$B$3),$A14*(1-$B$4)))) | |
| 15 | | | | | |

(This is why IFS is so beautiful, because that looks pretty scary, doesn't it? I'm having flashbacks to learning how to use a slide rule in 9th grade. Like, why? But trust me that this can be useful to learn.)

Let's break this down step by step.

What is the first part of this formula?

$$=IF(\$A8<\$A\$2,$$

Okay. So we have an IF function. What question is this asking?

$$\$A8<\$A\$2$$

"Is the value in Cell A8 (our customer purchase price), less than the value in Cell A2 (our first discount cutoff)?"

Always be careful with your edge cases. Does $25 earn a discount? Or do you have to be over $25?

Here I was fine because $25 earns a discount so we want to ask if we're under that.

Okay. So we have the first question we're asking. Note the dollar signs for any reference to the discount table so we only have to write this once and can then just copy it down. (Honestly, I write it first and then go back and put in the dollar signs.)

What do we want Excel to do if the value in Cell A8 is less than the value in Cell A2?

The answer is whatever is after that comma and before the next one:

$$\$A8$$

If the purchase amount is less than our first discount level, then it says to return the purchase amount. Makes sense. So far so good.

Here's where it gets "fun". What do we want Excel to do if that isn't the case? The entire rest of the formula:

$$IF(\$A8<\$A\$3,\$A8*(1-\$B\$2),IF(\$A8<\$A\$4,\$A8*(1-\$B\$3),\$A8*(1-\$B\$4)))$$

Yikes! That's a lot.

But really it's just the rest of the flow chart. So what is the next step saying?

$$IF(\$A8<\$A\$3$$

Is the value in Cell A8 that we already know is $25 or more, less than the value in Cell A3 (our second discount cutoff)?

If it is, then what?

$$\$A8*(1-\$B\$2)$$

Then take the customer purchase price in Cell A8, and multiply it by one minus the value in Cell B2, which is the corresponding discount rate if you get to $25.

Note that's B2 not B3. Because if our customer purchase price is less than our second discount threshold, we want to give the customer the first-level discount.

And we do one minus that value, because we're taking off 10% for the customer. They still need to pay 90% of the original purchase price. (You could simplify your IF function by putting 90% into the table and doing the math in advance if you wanted, but I prefer to do it this way.)

Okay. What if our customer purchase price is *not* under that second discount cutoff? Then we have the remainder of the formula to work through:

$$IF(\$A8<\$A\$4,\$A8*(1-\$B\$3),\$A8*(1-\$B\$4))))$$

It still looks pretty ugly, but now we're down to a simple IF function with two extra parens at the end to close out the first two IF functions.

I like to write nested IF functions this way because they're easier to close out. You can also write a nested IF function that builds from the center outward instead, but then you have to put each closing paren in the midst of the formula, which is more error prone.

If your formula generates an error message, look for missing parens or commas first. That's usually going to be your problem. Also, one way to troubleshoot a complex nested IF function is to replace the messiness with a placeholder. That whole original formula becomes:

$$=IF(\$A8<\$A\$2,\$A8,ELSE)$$

You can then ask, does that make sense? If it does, then you can look at the ELSE part separately.

Okay, now on to IFS which is the newer, better way to write conditional formulas that have more than two outcomes.

# The IFS Function

**Notation:** IFS(logical_test1, value_if_true1,…)

**Excel Definition:** Checks whether one or more conditions are met and returns a value corresponding to the first TRUE condition.

Technically, the IFS function can completely replace the IF function, but I still prefer to use IF for simple THIS-or-THAT comparisons. Where IFS really shines is when applied to multi-step IF-THEN-ELSE IF-THEN-ELSE type analysis.

The notation only shows you two inputs for IFS: what question you're asking (logical_test1) and the value if that's true (value_if_true1), but for me it really takes more inputs than that to do what I do with IF or IFS.

Let's go back to that first IF example we had where we wanted to keep a cell blank when there was no number to divide by.

Here it is:

$$=IF(C1="","",B1/C1)$$

Take a moment and try to think how you could convert that to an IFS function. According to the notation there, you only need two inputs:

$$=IFS(C1="","")$$

That is a working function. You will get a result. But there's no calculation. Could you get it to do a calculation with just two inputs?

Maybe one of these works:

$$=IFS(C1<>0,B1/C1)$$

$$=IFS(NOT(ISBLANK(C1)),B1/C1)$$

The first one is saying that if Cell C1 is not equal to zero, do your calculation. The second uses two functions we haven't covered yet. It basically says that if Cell C1 is not blank then do the calculation. Problem is, both of those return #N/A when Cell C1 doesn't have a value in it.

So really, not what I want. To use IFS in the way I want, I need to give Excel more.

When you add one more comma to one of these IFS functions, Excel's going to show you that you need to start adding additional inputs in pairs:

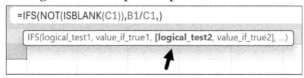

It puts logical_test2, value_if_true2 in the same set of brackets. Meaning if you add one, you have to add the other.

So how would you do that. Because all we really wanted was to do the calculation, right? We wanted to take this

$$=IFS(C1="","")$$

and add one more input for the calculation, but it wants two inputs.

(Do you hate me yet for not just explaining? Yeah, sorry. Trying to keep you awake.)

Here's the answer:

$$=IFS(C1="","",TRUE,B1/C1)$$

We add a new test that you can't fail. TRUE. TRUE is TRUE. And if that's the case, then do the calculation.

So we end up with a formula that basically says, "If Cell C1 is blank, then return a blank value, otherwise, if TRUE is TRUE, which it always is, divide the value in Cell B1 by the value in Cell C1."

I made you walk through this thought process in the hopes that it would stick better for you, because I do not find it intuitive. I always need to remember that my last input is not just, "do the thing", it's a final test that can't be failed, and *then* "do the thing".

You may be wondering why Excel does this. Can't they just default it somehow? And maybe they could've if they'd listed "final result" as the *second* input, but they didn't build it that way. It probably would've been a little counterintuitive. So you have to put TRUE (or some other test that can't be failed) as your final logical test to let Excel know you're done.

Just for kicks, I just tried setting the last test to 2=2, like so:

$$=IFS(C1="","",2=2,B1/C1)$$

and that worked, too.

Excel doesn't know how long your decision tree is, so that final logical test is how you stop.

If you don't give the IFS function a stopping point and none of your prior criteria are met, you'll get a #N/A error message.

Okay, you probably hate IFS right now. But let's go back to our complicated nested IF function and replace it with an IFS function. For those of you who skipped that section, don't worry, just notice how complex this is and that it uses three different IF functions nested together to get results:

$$=IF(\$A8<\$A\$2,\$A8,IF(\$A8<\$A\$3,\$A8*(1-\$B\$2),IF(\$A8<\$A\$4,\$A8*(1-\$B\$3),\$A8*(1-\$B\$4))))$$

Here is that discount table but now using IFS to calculate discounts:

| | A | B | C | D | E |
|---|---|---|---|---|---|
| 1 | Purchase Amount | Discount Percent | | | |
| 2 | $25.00 | 10% | | | |
| 3 | $50.00 | 20% | | | |
| 4 | $75.00 | 25% | | | |
| 5 | | | | | |
| 6 | | | | | |
| 7 | Customer Purchases | Price after Discount | | Formula | |
| 8 | $25.00 | $22.50 | | =IFS($A8<$A$2,$A8,$A8<$A$3,$A8*(1-$B$2),$A8<$A$4,$A8*(1-$B$3),TRUE,$A8*(1-$B$4)) | |
| 9 | $50.00 | $40.00 | | =IFS($A9<$A$2,$A9,$A9<$A$3,$A9*(1-$B$2),$A9<$A$4,$A9*(1-$B$3),TRUE,$A9*(1-$B$4)) | |
| 10 | $75.00 | $56.25 | | =IFS($A10<$A$2,$A10,$A10<$A$3,$A10*(1-$B$2),$A10<$A$4,$A10*(1-$B$3),TRUE,$A10*(1-$B$4)) | |
| 11 | $15.00 | $15.00 | | =IFS($A11<$A$2,$A11,$A11<$A$3,$A11*(1-$B$2),$A11<$A$4,$A11*(1-$B$3),TRUE,$A11*(1-$B$4)) | |
| 12 | $60.00 | $48.00 | | =IFS($A12<$A$2,$A12,$A12<$A$3,$A12*(1-$B$2),$A12<$A$4,$A12*(1-$B$3),TRUE,$A12*(1-$B$4)) | |
| 13 | $80.00 | $60.00 | | =IFS($A13<$A$2,$A13,$A13<$A$3,$A13*(1-$B$2),$A13<$A$4,$A13*(1-$B$3),TRUE,$A13*(1-$B$4)) | |
| 14 | $40.00 | $36.00 | | =IFS($A14<$A$2,$A14,$A14<$A$3,$A14*(1-$B$2),$A14<$A$4,$A14*(1-$B$3),TRUE,$A14*(1-$B$4)) | |
| 15 | | | | | |

And here is the formula for Row 8. Still lengthy, but much easier to write. Let's walk through it.

$$=IFS(\$A8<\$A\$2,\$A8,\$A8<\$A\$3,\$A8*(1-\$B\$2),\$A8<\$A\$4,\$A8*(1-\$B\$3),TRUE,\$A8*(1-\$B\$4))$$

First, let's remove all the dollar signs, which only matter if you want to copy it:

$$=IFS(A8<A2,A8,A8<A3,A8*(1-B2),A8<A4,A8*(1-B3),TRUE,A8*(1-B4))$$

Step one of the formula asks a question:

$$IFS(A8<A2$$

Is the value in Cell A8 less than the value in Cell A2?
Step two tells you what to do if the answer is Yes:

$$A8$$

Return the full customer purchase price from Cell A8.
That's pretty much what the IF function version does, too.
Step three is where things get simpler. Instead of using another IF function, we can just ask another question:

$$A8<A3$$

Is the value in A8 less than the value in A3?
The task to perform if that's the case is:

$$A8*(1-B2)$$

Apply the discount percent in Cell B2 to the value in Cell A8.
Next up is another question and task if true:

$$A8<A4,A8*(1-B3)$$

Is the value in Cell A8 less than the value in Cell A4? Apply the discount in Cell B3 if so.

And then our final question and task if true, which it better be, because our question was the answer, TRUE:

$$TRUE,A8*(1-B4)$$

Apply the highest discount to all remaining purchases.

I know it still feels complex to walk through an example like this, but trust me when I tell you it's much easier to write it.

If you ever get stuck with IFS, it's probably going to be because you asked the wrong questions or told Excel to perform the wrong tasks (rather than a missing paren or comma which is often the issue with IF). So if you aren't getting the right result, draw it out and replace the questions with the cell references that ask the questions.

Like so:

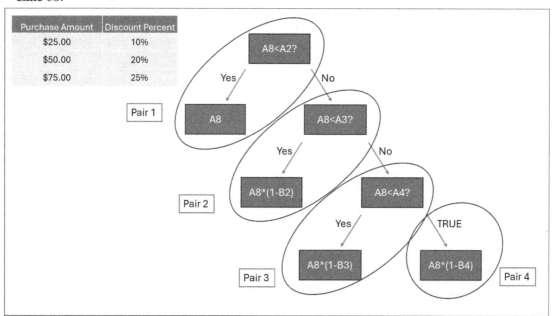

You can then check your IFS function against each paired set, circled in the diagram above.

Alright. That was a lot. If you're reading this book straight through, stand up, stretch, take a walk, take a nap, take a break.

(Honestly, sometimes getting a good night's sleep after you first learn something hard, is the best way to give your mind the time to process and absorb what you learned. Trust me. Sleep is better than all night cram sessions. Just, you know, at least read the material once before you go to sleep.)

# The IFNA Function

**Notation:** IFNA(value, value_if_na)

**Excel Definition:** Returns the value you specify if the expression resolves to #N/A, otherwise returns the result of the expression.

The IFNA function basically lets you suppress a #N/A result so that it isn't visible. Going back to our divided by zero IFS example from the last chapter:

=IFS(C1<>0,B1/C1)

I could take that and surround it with IFNA to keep it from showing the #N/A error message when C1 is empty or equal to zero:

=IFNA(IFS(C1<>0,B1/C1),"")

If you leave the value_if_na blank it will return a value of zero:

=IFNA(IFS(C1<>0,B1/C1),)

You can also have it return text:

=IFNA(IFS(C1<>0,B1/C1),"Not applicable")

One more thing to keep in mind with IFNA is that the only error type it suppresses is the #N/A error. So if I had

=IFNA(B2/C2,"Not applicable")

and C2 was blank, I would still see the #DIV/0! error message. The reason to use it instead of IFERROR, which we'll cover next, is it doesn't hide important error messages you do need to see like #REF!

# The IFERROR Function

**Notation:** IFERROR(value, value_if_error)

**Excel Definition:** Returns value_if_error if expression is an error and the value of the expression itself otherwise.

IFERROR works just like IFNA except it suppresses more error messages. It will suppress #N/A, #REF!, #VALUE!, #NUM!, #NAME?, #NULL!, and #DIV/0!

It also works with array functions just fine. (As does IFNA.) With an array function, if there are no errors, you'll still get all of your results, but if there are any errors in the range you'll get whatever you specified for value_if_error. You can see this by using:

$$=IFERROR((RANDARRAY(2,4)/0),"Issue")$$

That should generate a two by four grid of cells with the word "Issue" in them.

IFERROR does not suppress a #SPILL! error. You can see that by typing something in one of the fields that has the "Issue" result in that last example.

# The AND Function

**Notation:** AND(logical1, [logical2],…)

**Excel Definition:** Checks whether all arguments are TRUE, and returns TRUE if all arguments are TRUE.

Technically, you just need one input for this function to work, the first logical statement, but I almost always have at least two.

I don't think I've ever used the AND function by itself. You could. You could have it evaluate all of your criteria are met, but usually I am asking a question like that because I want to do something with the answer. Which is why I usually combine this function with an IF or IFS function.

Let's walk through an example.

One of the places I publish my ebooks is on Amazon. For as long as I've been publishing with them, they've had different payouts for different price points. If you're under $2.99 (USD) they pay 35%. They also pay 35% if you're over $9.99. In between $2.99 and $9.99 they pay 70%. Which means that to earn 70% you need to both be greater than or equal to $2.99 AND less than or equal to $9.99.

So we have two questions that need to be TRUE to earn 70%.

The first one: Is my price greater than or equal to $2.99? If the value is in Cell A1, that would be written as:

$$A1>=2.99$$

You can put that into the AND function as a single input

$$=AND(A1>=2.99)$$

If the value in Cell A1 is greater than or equal to 2.99 we will get a TRUE result. If it's less than 2.99 we will get a FALSE result.

But that's not really an "and" sort of evaluation, even though we used the AND function for it.

So let's add our second question. Is the value in Cell A1 less than or equal to 9.99?

$$A1<=9.99$$

Add that to our AND function and we get:

$$=AND(A1>=2.99,A1<=9.99)$$

For this to return a value of TRUE, the number in Cell A1 has to be both greater than or equal to $2.99 AND less than or equal to 9.99.

Here I've taken a range of values, $3.99, $0.99, $10.99, $2.99, and $9.99. For all of them I've applied the AND formula from above that includes both criteria. For the ones that aren't our edge case I've also used AND formulas that look at just one of the two criteria at a time:

| | A | B | C |
|---|---|---|---|
| 1 | **Value** | **AND Result** | **AND Formula** |
| 2 | $3.99 | TRUE | =AND(A2>=2.99) |
| 3 | $3.99 | TRUE | =AND(A3<=9.99) |
| 4 | $3.99 | TRUE | =AND(A4>=2.99,A4<=9.99) |
| 5 | $0.99 | FALSE | =AND(A5>=2.99) |
| 6 | $0.99 | TRUE | =AND(A6<=9.99) |
| 7 | $0.99 | FALSE | =AND(A7>=2.99,A7<=9.99) |
| 8 | $10.99 | TRUE | =AND(A8>=2.99) |
| 9 | $10.99 | FALSE | =AND(A9<=9.99) |
| 10 | $10.99 | FALSE | =AND(A10>=2.99,A10<=9.99) |
| 11 | $2.99 | TRUE | =AND(A11>=2.99,A11<=9.99) |
| 12 | $9.99 | TRUE | =AND(A12>=2.99,A12<=9.99) |
| 13 | | | |

Column A has the values to evaluate, Column B has the TRUE/FALSE result, and Column C shows the formula used in that row.

Rows 2 through 4 evaluate $3.99, and since $3.99 is both greater than $2.99 and less than $9.99, we get TRUE for all three formulas.

Rows 5 through 7 evaluate $0.99. In this case, the value is not over $2.99, so that returns a FALSE, which means our combined AND formula does as well.

Rows 8 through 10 evaluate $10.99. Since this value is over $9.99, that AND function returns a FALSE result, which means the combined formula does as well.

Make sense? Individual parts of an AND function can be TRUE, but if everything isn't TRUE, the AND function will return a result of FALSE.

Finally, in Rows 11 and 12 we have the two edge cases, $2.99 and $9.99, to make sure the combined AND statement returns the correct result.

Now let's combine AND with an IF function. This table takes various price points and calculates the payout at various price points:

| | F | G | H | |
|---|---|---|---|---|
| 1 | Value | IF(AND) Result | IF(AND) Formula | |
| 2 | $0.99 | $0.35 | =IF(AND(F2>=2.99,F2<=9.99),F2*0.7,F2*0.35) | |
| 3 | $2.99 | $2.09 | =IF(AND(F3>=2.99,F3<=9.99),F3*0.7,F3*0.35) | |
| 4 | $3.99 | $2.79 | =IF(AND(F4>=2.99,F4<=9.99),F4*0.7,F4*0.35) | |
| 5 | $9.99 | $6.99 | =IF(AND(F5>=2.99,F5<=9.99),F5*0.7,F5*0.35) | |
| 6 | $10.99 | $3.85 | =IF(AND(F6>=2.99,F6<=9.99),F6*0.7,F6*0.35) | |
| 7 | | | | |

Column F has the prices, Column G has the result, and Column H has the formula. For Row 2 the formula is:

$$=IF(AND(F2>=2.99,F2<=9.99),F2*0.7,F2*0.35)$$

This formula starts with IF, so we know that we have two possible outcomes. The first one is:

$$AND(F2>=2.99,F2<=9.99)$$

Is the value in Cell F2 both greater than or equal to $2.99 AND less than or equal to $9.99? If so, then:

$$F2*0.7$$

Multiply the price by 70% to get the payout.
If not, then:

$$F2*0.35$$

Multiply the price by 35%.

Now. For the overachievers, I actually used a slightly different formula than that, because I only wanted two decimal places in my results.

The formula I actually used was:

$$=ROUND(IF(AND(F2>=2.99,F2<=9.99),F2*0.7,F2*0.35),2)$$

That looks really complex until you replace the IF function with an X:

$$=ROUND(X,2)$$

So basically I just surrounded our IF function with a ROUND function because the actual results were numbers like 3.8465 and I wanted currency results instead.

# The OR Function

**Notation:** OR(logical1, [logical2],…)

**Excel Definition:** Checks whether any of the arguments are TRUE, and returns TRUE or FALSE. Returns FALSE only if all arguments are FALSE.

The OR function works much like the AND function, except you will get a TRUE result if any of the inputs you provide the function are true.

Let's go back to our Amazon payout example. We could write a formula that uses the OR function instead, as long as we realize that Amazon pays 35% if a book is priced under $2.99 OR if it is priced over $9.99.

Here's our first table of prices we could charge, but with OR now:

| | A | B | C |
|---|---|---|---|
| 1 | **Value** | **OR Result** | **OR Formula** |
| 2 | $3.99 | FALSE | =OR(A2<2.99) |
| 3 | $3.99 | FALSE | =OR(A3>9.99) |
| 4 | $3.99 | FALSE | =OR(A4<2.99,A4>9.99) |
| 5 | $0.99 | TRUE | =OR(A5<2.99) |
| 6 | $0.99 | FALSE | =OR(A6>9.99) |
| 7 | $0.99 | TRUE | =OR(A7<2.99,A7>9.99) |
| 8 | $10.99 | FALSE | =OR(A8<2.99) |
| 9 | $10.99 | TRUE | =OR(A9>9.99) |
| 10 | $10.99 | TRUE | =OR(A10<2.99,A10>9.99) |
| 11 | $2.99 | FALSE | =OR(A11<2.99,A11>9.99) |
| 12 | $9.99 | FALSE | =OR(A12<2.99,A12>9.99) |
| 13 | | | |

Rows 2 through 4 still use $3.99, but now all three of those are FALSE. This value is not less than $2.99, nor is it greater than $9.99, which means the combined result:

$$=OR(A4<2.99,A4>9.99)$$

is also FALSE.

Rows 5 through 7 still use 99 cents. Row 5 is TRUE because it is less than $2.99. Row 6 is FALSE because it is not greater than $9.99. The combined formula is also TRUE because only one of the two conditions needs to be met.

Okay. Now on to the IF function wrapped around an OR function:

| | F | G | H |
|---|---|---|---|
| 1 | **Value** | **IF(OR) Result** | **IF(OR) Formula** |
| 2 | $0.99 | $0.35 | =IF(OR(F2<2.99,F2>9.99),F2*0.35,F2*0.7) |
| 3 | $2.99 | $2.09 | =IF(OR(F3<2.99,F3>9.99),F3*0.35,F3*0.7) |
| 4 | $3.99 | $2.79 | =IF(OR(F4<2.99,F4>9.99),F4*0.35,F4*0.7) |
| 5 | $9.99 | $6.99 | =IF(OR(F5<2.99,F5>9.99),F5*0.35,F5*0.7) |
| 6 | $10.99 | $3.85 | =IF(OR(F6<2.99,F6>9.99),F6*0.35,F6*0.7) |
| 7 | | | |

Let's look at the formula for Row 2:

$$=IF(OR(F2<2.99,F2>9.99),F2*0.35,F2*0.7)$$

That is saying, if the price in Cell F2 is less than 2.99 OR greater than 9.99, then multiply it by 35%, otherwise multiply it by 70%.

So we had to swap where we did the multiplying by .35 and by .7, because the TRUE outcome here means the lower payout. But we get what we need this way just as easily as we did with AND.

So to recap: Use AND when there are multiple criteria that all have to be met. Use OR when any one of the criteria must be met but you don't have to meet them all.

Finally, I was using cell references for these examples to make it easy, but all of the criteria we covered in the SUMIFS chapter can be used here. You can use text, date, or number criteria.

# The ISBLANK Function

**Notation:** ISBLANK(value)

**Excel Definition:** Checks whether a reference is to an empty cell, and returns TRUE or FALSE.

What ISBLANK does is looks at the cell or cell range you provide, and tells you whether the cell or cells in the range are blank.

Blank means no text or formula or "" result. It has to be truly blank.

It doesn't pick up formatting, so that's fine, but it will give a FALSE result if there is a formula in that cell, or if you had a null result returned that you copy pasted – special values.

If you run into Excel saying that a cell that looks blank is not blank, you can use Clear Contents in the Editing section of the Home tab to truly clear that cell of any content.

If you use a cell range, ISBLANK will return an array result equal to the size of the selected range, and will provide a distinct result for each cell in the range.

This is one of those functions that on its own you probably won't use often. Maybe to troubleshoot some data that isn't working the way it looks like it should. For example, maybe COUNTA is returning a count even though there's nothing to see.

It's more likely you'll use it to trigger an IFS or IF function like I did with the two examples earlier in this book. Here's the one I used with TEXTJOIN to help determine when to use different sets of delimiters:

=IFS(**ISBLANK**(D16),TEXTJOIN($G$21:$G$22,TRUE,A16:D16),**ISBLANK**(B16), TEXTJOIN($G$21:$G$22,TRUE,A16:D16),TRUE,TEXTJOIN($G$20:$G$22,TRUE,A16: D16))

And here's the one I used with IFS to say only do this calculation if Cell C1 is not blank.

=IFS(NOT(**ISBLANK**(C1)),B1/C1)

# The NOT Function

**Notation:** NOT(logical)

**Excel Definition:** Changes FALSE to TRUE, or TRUE to FALSE

Before this week I would've told you that I have yet to find a good use for the NOT function. Because it's basically a function that takes a result, like TRUE, and replaces it with its opposite, FALSE. I can usually find a better way to do that. For example, the help on this one has a sales commission calculation that I could do much easier in other ways.

But earlier in this book, I actually reached for NOT to write a formula for you, so I figured I should include it.

Here's the formula again.

$$=IFS(\textbf{NOT}(ISBLANK(C1)),B1/C1)$$

What is this doing:

$$NOT(ISBLANK(C1))$$

By surrounding ISBLANK with NOT we're basically asking if there's something in that cell. That is a nice, legitimate use of NOT that I can get behind because as I write this I am not aware of the existence of a "not blank" counterpart to ISBLANK.

I do expect that when you get into writing macros in Excel—which are littles scripts to get Excel to perform complex tasks for you—that this one could come up more often. But for normal, everyday people like you and me, I'd say the uses are pretty limited.

But if you are ever thinking to yourself, "Gosh, I wish I could take this yes/no question I asked and turn it into its opposite," this is how you'd do that.

Okay. On to something more useful, XLOOKUP. And closing in on the end of this book. (Aren't you excited?)

# The XLOOKUP Function

**Notation:** XLOOKUP(lookup_value, lookup_array, return_array, [if_not_found], [match_mode], [search_mode])

**Excel Definition:** Searches a range or an array for a match and returns the corresponding item from a second range or array. By default, an exact match is used.

I love this function so much I'm pretty sure I proposed marriage to whoever created it in one of my books. (Not seriously, of course. That would be the bad kind of weird and none of us want to be that.)

Anyway. XLOOKUP lets you take a value, the lookup_value, and then look in a range of cells, the lookup_array, to return a result from a designated range of cells that match up to the lookup array, the return_array.

Your lookup array and your return array can be the same, but they will often be different. For example, you'll look up customer number and want to return customer name.

The other inputs into the XLOOKUP function are optional. They let you tell Excel what to do if there is no match found, whether to match exactly or find the closest result (which is often helpful when you use the same lookup and return array), and how to search.

This is a newer function, so a lot of people aren't using it yet. You may instead stumble upon the VLOOKUP function, which I'll cover in the next chapter. But trust me when I tell you, that this is the function you want to use if at all possible.

Okay. So examples.

Let's start with an exact match example. Here is a table of customer transaction information:

| | A | B | C | D | E |
|---|---|---|---|---|---|
| 1 | Date | Customer | Product | Units | Total Cost |
| 2 | 2/6/2020 | 123456 | Widget | 14 | $ 31.50 |
| 3 | 2/25/2020 | 78542 | Whatchamacallit | 3 | $ 33.75 |
| 4 | 4/1/2020 | 698124 | Widget | 8 | $ 18.00 |
| 5 | 4/7/2020 | 12793 | Whatchamacallit | 11 | $ 123.75 |
| 6 | 4/25/2020 | 3267 | Whatsit | 11 | $ 14.85 |
| 7 | 4/28/2020 | 4937 | Widget | 9 | $ 20.25 |

Who is customer 78542? We can go manually look in our customer data table to see it's Shane Morales:

| | G | H | I |
|---|---|---|---|
| 1 | Customer Number | Customer Last Name | Customer First Name |
| 2 | 3267 | Gutierrez | Luisa |
| 3 | 4937 | Holsen | Gary |
| 4 | 12793 | Phong | Bob |
| 5 | 78542 | Morales | Shane |
| 6 | 123456 | Lee | John |
| 7 | 698124 | Jones | Sheila |

But what if we want to do this for a thousand transactions? That would be annoying. That's where XLOOKUP can come in handy. We can take the customer number in the first table, look it up in the second table, and then pull the first and last name of each customer. Let's build this for first name.

The first input is what we are looking up.

I want to look up the customer account number in Cell B2, so I start with:

=XLOOKUP(B2,

Next, where am I looking for this?

In my case, all of my information is in the same worksheet and the customer information table has account numbers in Column G, so I can write:

=XLOOKUP(B2,G:G,

If it were in a different worksheet, I'd just go to that worksheet and click on the column that had customer number in it and end up with something like

=XLOOKUP(B2,'Customer Data'!G:G,

The next input is what information we want to pull. First name results are in Column I for me, so that's what I'll use. I could stop there. Everything past that point is optional and I'm okay with the defaults. That would get me:

=XLOOKUP(B2,G:G,I:I)

But let's keep going.

The next input is what to put if there is no listing for what you're looking for. The default is to return #N/A. If you want it to return text, put the text in quotes. Like so:

=XLOOKUP(B3,G:G,I:I,"Unknown Customer Number")

This would return the text "Unknown Customer Number" if there wasn't an exact match between the number I'm looking up and the table I'm looking in.

The next optional input is match_mode. You have four options. If you use zero, 0, Excel looks for an exact match. This is the default option. Your other match choices are -1, which looks for an exact match but will go to the next smaller item in the list if there is no exact match, 1, which looks for an exact match but will go to the next higher item in the list if there isn't an exact match, and 2, which is a wildcard character match.

To use 2, the lookup value you use needs to contain a * or ? wildcard. If I looked for "*Jones", this would tell Excel to match to something like "A Jones".

(Also, just a note as I was playing with this, that Excel treated "Jones" and "Jones " the same for search purposes. It didn't treat that extra space as making the value different. It seems sometimes Excel does and sometimes it doesn't, so you kind of have to test it for search, filter, or functions.)

Okay, so in this instance we want an exact match. We could just put a comma and no number or we can put 0.

=XLOOKUP(B3,G:G,I:I,"Unknown Customer Number",0)

The final input is how to search the list. For an exact match it shouldn't matter what you use.

The two main choices are 1 to search first-to-last and -1 to search last-to-first. Excel does the heavy lifting behind the scenes for those two choices, and puts everything in order for you.

There are other options, but they both require that the lookup_array already be sorted. 2 will search your list assuming the data is sorted in ascending order, and -2 will search assuming the data is sorted in descending order. Do not use them if your data is not sorted properly, and you're trying to find the closest value. You will get an incorrect result.

One more really cool thing to share, and then we'll do a more complex example:

You can have Excel return more than one value at a time for you. For example, in my advertising spreadsheet I have Excel look up the title of my book in a list that then lets it return the author name, the series name, and the official identifier for that book. I used to use three separate formulas to do this, but with XLOOKUP I can do it with one.

Let's go back to our example above:

$$=XLOOKUP(B2,G:G,I:I)$$

If I wanted to return both last name and first name from our customer table at the same time, I would simply list the column range as my last input:

$$=XLOOKUP(B2,G:G,H:I)$$

That assumes, of course, that I want Column H returned before Column I. If I want Column I first and then Column H, I couldn't use this trick, I'd need separate formulas for each lookup array. (And I did try curly brackets on this one and they won't work. So your columns have to be in the same order or you have to write the formulas one lookup array at a time.)

Okay.

Now let's go through an example where we don't want an exact match by revisiting the discount table we used for the IFS function.

I had to make one edit, which was to add a row for no discount. Here we go:

| | A | B | C | D | E |
|---|---|---|---|---|---|
| 1 | **Purchase Amount** | **Discount Percent** | | | |
| 2 | $0.00 | 0% | | | |
| 3 | $25.00 | 10% | | | |
| 4 | $50.00 | 20% | | | |
| 5 | $75.00 | 25% | | | |
| 6 | | | | | |
| 7 | | | | | |
| 8 | **Customer Purchases** | **Price after Discount** | | **Formula** | |
| 9 | $25.00 | $22.50 | =$A9*(1-XLOOKUP($A9,$A$2:$A$5,$B$2:$B$5,,-1,1)) | | |
| 10 | $50.00 | $40.00 | =$A10*(1-XLOOKUP($A10,$A$2:$A$5,$B$2:$B$5,,-1,1)) | | |
| 11 | $75.00 | $56.25 | =$A11*(1-XLOOKUP($A11,$A$2:$A$5,$B$2:$B$5,,-1,1)) | | |
| 12 | $15.00 | $15.00 | =$A12*(1-XLOOKUP($A12,$A$2:$A$5,$B$2:$B$5,,-1,1)) | | |
| 13 | $60.00 | $48.00 | =$A13*(1-XLOOKUP($A13,$A$2:$A$5,$B$2:$B$5,,-1,1)) | | |
| 14 | $80.00 | $60.00 | =$A14*(1-XLOOKUP($A14,$A$2:$A$5,$B$2:$B$5,,-1,1)) | | |
| 15 | $40.00 | $36.00 | =$A15*(1-XLOOKUP($A15,$A$2:$A$5,$B$2:$B$5,,-1,1)) | | |
| 16 | | | | | |

That's a lot to absorb. Let's look at the formula in Row 9:

$$=\$A9*(1-XLOOKUP(\$A9,\$A\$2:\$A\$5,\$B\$2:\$B\$5,,-1,1))$$

Those dollar signs are all there to fix cell references to make it easy to copy, so let's take them out for now:

$$=A9*(1-XLOOKUP(A9,A2:A5,B2:B5,,-1,1))$$

Real quick, I want to show you what happens when I replace the entire XLOOKUP function with X:

$$=A9*(1-X)$$

So what this is really doing is having XLOOKUP pull a discount percentage for us. Great. How is it doing that?

XLOOKUP(A9,A2:A5,B2:B5,,-1,1)

The first input, what to look up, is Cell A9. That's the customer's purchase price.

The next input is our lookup array, Cells A2 through A5. Those are the dollar values for the discount thresholds. Think about that one for a moment. We're not going to have exact matches to those values most of the time. So how would you use those cutoffs? (Hold that thought for now.)

The third input, is our return array, Cells B2 through B5. So we're pulling the discount percentages based on the discount thresholds.

With me so far?

The next input is blank. That's what we'd return if there was a failed lookup. I don't expect to have that, so I'm fine with a default #N/A error message. (Which did happen the first time I ran this. Because I'd forgotten to add that Row 2 that has 0 and 0% and it's needed for this to work.)

The fifth input is very important. I used -1.

That says, "Look for my purchase price. If you can't find an exact match to the purchase price, then drop back to the next lowest value."

So if I have $37.50, I want Excel to drop back to the discount percent for $25. We didn't reach the $50 discount level, we have to go back to the one we did reach.

I used 1 for the final input here, but I didn't need it. My data is sorted in ascending order, so the only option that wouldn't work is -2.

Excel went through for each of my values, looked for the customer's purchase price, compared it to the discount table, and gave the discount percent that the customer had reached. I needed that $0 level for it to have somewhere to drop back to when a customer hadn't reached the first discount threshold.

Great, so that worked.

But where I think XLOOKUP really shines, is with data that is messier. Let's look at an example.

In the table on the next page, Rows 1 through 9 are our data set, which contains information about different books, author, series, title, wordcount, hours to write, and genre.

The unique value that we can look up, Title, is in Column C. There can be duplicates in the other columns, such as author name or series name, but there is only one example of each Title in this table.

I want to look for author name (in Column A) and series (in Column B) for each title.

How would you do that?

You can see how I did it in Rows 12 through 14. The formula I used for Title H is in Row 12:

=XLOOKUP(A12,C2:C9,A2:B9,,0,1)

| | A | B | C | D | E | F |
|---|---|---|---|---|---|---|
| 1 | Author Name | Related Series | Title | Wordcount | Hours to Write | Genre |
| 2 | Author A | Series A | Title A | 26,527 | 26.5 | Non-Fiction |
| 3 | Author A | Series C | Title C | 7,893 | 6 | Non-Fiction |
| 4 | Author A | Series C | Title E | 4,997 | 4 | Non-Fiction |
| 5 | Author A | Series C | Title F | 7,976 | 4.25 | Non-Fiction |
| 6 | Author A | Series C | Title G | 57,900 | 23 | Non-Fiction |
| 7 | Author A | Series A | Title H | 8,284 | 5.75 | Non-Fiction |
| 8 | Author B | Series B | Title B | 46,204 | 54.25 | Spec Fiction |
| 9 | Author B | Series B | | 6,079 | 4 | Spec Fiction |
| 10 | | | | | | |
| 11 | Value | Formula | | | Result | |
| 12 | Title H | =XLOOKUP($A12,$C$2:$C$9,$A$2:$B$9,,0,1) | | | Author A | Series A |
| 13 | Title E | =XLOOKUP($A13,$C$2:$C$9,$A$2:$B$9,,0,1) | | | Author A | Series C |
| 14 | Title B | =XLOOKUP($A14,$C$2:$C$9,$A$2:$B$9,,0,1) | | | Author B | Series B |
| 15 | | | | | | |

That says, look for the value in Cell A12, Title H, in Cells C2 through C9. When you find an exact match, pull the values in Columns A and B from the same row.

Because I wanted it to return results from both Columns A and B, the results show up in Cells E12 *and* F12. Cell E12 is where the actual formula that returns that result is. Since this is an array result, I would see a #SPILL! error in Cell E12 if there was already something in Cell F12.

One final cool thing that XLOOKUP can do (and that I always forget about), is return results between two points. If you combine it with SUM, it can return the sum of the result for a range of cells.

Here we go:

| | A | B | C | D | E | F | G | H |
|---|---|---|---|---|---|---|---|---|
| 1 | | Units Sold | | Start | End | Formula | Result | |
| 2 | January | 1,253 | | January | March | =XLOOKUP(D2,$A$2:$A$13,$A$2:$B$13):XLOOKUP(E2,$A$2:$A$13,$A$2:$B$13) | January | 1253 |
| 3 | February | 1,417 | | | | | February | 1417 |
| 4 | March | 1,406 | | | | | March | 1406 |
| 5 | April | 929 | | | | | | |
| 6 | May | 850 | | January | March | =SUM(XLOOKUP(D2,$A$2:$A$13,$A$2:$B$13):XLOOKUP(E2,$A$2:$A$13,$A$2:$B$13)) | 4076 | |
| 7 | June | 965 | | | | | | |
| 8 | July | 736 | | | | | | |
| 9 | August | 660 | | | | | | |
| 10 | September | 710 | | | | | | |
| 11 | October | 1,041 | | | | | | |
| 12 | November | 942 | | | | | | |
| 13 | December | 1,159 | | | | | | |
| 14 | | | | | | | | |

Columns A and B have total units sold for each month for a year. Column A has the month, Column B has the number of units sold.

In Rows 2 through 4 of Columns G and H, I have sales results for January, February, and March. These are there as the result of the XLOOKUP function you can see in Cell F2 that was used in Cell G2.

Let's look at it in closer detail:

=XLOOKUP(D2,$A$2:$A$13,$A$2:$B$13):XLOOKUP(E2,$A$2:$A$13,$A$2:$B$13)

That looks complicated, but split it at the colon and you get two XLOOKUP functions:

XLOOKUP(D2,$A$2:$A$13,$A$2:$B$13)

XLOOKUP(E2,$A$2:$A$13,$A$2:$B$13)

One is looking up the value in Cell D2, which is January. The other is looking up the value in Cell E2, which is March. That colon is basically saying "through".

So Excel pulls the results not just for January and March, but for any months between them. In this case, just February, and returns an array result in Cells G2 through H4.

In Cell G6, I took that formula and wrapped it inside a SUM function. You can see the formula I used in Cell F6:

=SUM(XLOOKUP(D2,$A$2:$A$13,$A$2:$B$13):XLOOKUP(E2,$A$2:$A$13,$A$2:$B $13))

Once more, it looks messy, but it's basically

=SUM(X)

Where X is the individual results from the XLOOKUP functions we just discussed, which returned the number of units sold for January *through* March.

Pretty cool, huh?

One more for you:

| | A | B | C | D | E | F | G | H |
|---|---|---|---|---|---|---|---|---|
| 1 | | Units Sold | | Start | End | Formula | Result | |
| 2 | January | 1,253 | | January | December | =XLOOKUP(D2,$A$2:$A$13,$A$2:$B$13):XLOOKUP(E2,$A$2:$A$13,$A$2:$B$13) | January | 1253 |
| 3 | February | 1,417 | | | | | February | 1417 |
| 4 | March | 1,406 | | | | | March | 1406 |
| 5 | April | 929 | | | | | April | 929 |
| 6 | May | 850 | | | | | May | 850 |
| 7 | June | 965 | | | | | June | 965 |
| 8 | July | 736 | | | | | July | 736 |
| 9 | August | 660 | | | | | August | 660 |
| 10 | September | 710 | | | | | September | 710 |
| 11 | October | 1,041 | | | | | October | 1041 |
| 12 | November | 942 | | | | | November | 942 |
| 13 | December | 1,159 | | | | | December | 1159 |
| 14 | | | | | | | | |
| 15 | | | | January | December | =SUM(XLOOKUP(D2,$A$2:$A$13,$A$2:$B$13):XLOOKUP(E2,$A$2:$A$13,$A$2:$B$13)) | 12068 | |
| 16 | | | | | | | | |

All I did here was change the value in Cell E2 to December instead of March, and Excel pulled results for January *through* December.

Now, this worked because I have my months in the correct order. But if I move December to Cell A4, then Excel will stop at that point and not keep going. Using the colon basically says "pull the result for this first value and keep pulling results until you pull the result for the second value."

# The VLOOKUP Function

**Notation:** VLOOKUP(lookup_value, table_array, col_index_num, [range_lookup])

**Excel Definition:** Looks for a value in the leftmost column of a table, and then returns a value in the same row from a column you specify. By default, the table must be sorted in an ascending order.

I'm covering VLOOKUP here because you may still run into it at times, and it is important to know how it works so you can deal with it if you do. But both VLOOKUP (vertical lookup) and HLOOKUP (horizontal lookup) have been effectively replaced by XLOOKUP (lookup in any direction).

The first thing to notice is the start of the definition: "Looks for a value in the leftmost column of a table." Technically you could define your table as starting in the third column to get it to work, but the problem for me with VLOOKUP is that it can only pull results that are located in the lookup column or to the right of it.

So that example I had earlier where we looked up Title in Column C, and then returned author and series from Columns A and B? You can't do that with VLOOKUP. You'd have to change the order of the columns in the source table to use it.

Also, look at the end of that definition: "By default, the table must be sorted in an ascending order." VLOOKUP requires you to sort your data or it won't work properly. That's not an issue with an exact match, but it is an issue with the approximate match choice.

Since I am normally someone using Column C to pull data from Column A, and also working with data that isn't sorted, I kind of hate VLOOKUP. Fortunately, now that XLOOKUP exists, I never have to deal with it.

But as I've said more than once at this point, a lot of people really like VLOOKUP, which means that if you're ever working in an environment where other people have built your files, or where people have been working in Excel for a long time, you may run into it. So best to understand it.

Let's go back to my Title example:

| | A | B | C | D | E | F |
|---|---|---|---|---|---|---|
| 1 | Title | Author Name | Related Series | Wordcount | Hours to Write | Genre |
| 2 | Title H | Author A | Series A | 8,284 | 5.75 | Non-Fiction |
| 3 | Title F | Author A | Series C | 7,976 | 4.25 | Non-Fiction |
| 4 | Title A | Author A | Series A | 26,527 | 26.5 | Non-Fiction |
| 5 | Title C | Author A | Series C | 7,893 | 6 | Non-Fiction |
| 6 | Title E | Author A | Series C | 4,997 | 4 | Non-Fiction |
| 7 | Title G | Author A | Series C | 57,900 | 23 | Non-Fiction |
| 8 | Title B | Author B | Series B | 46,204 | 54.25 | Spec Fiction |
| 9 | | Author B | Series B | 6,079 | 4 | Spec Fiction |
| 10 | | | | | | |
| 11 | Value | Formula | | | Result | |
| 12 | Title H | =VLOOKUP($A12,$A$2:$F$9,{2,3},FALSE) | | | Author A | Series A |
| 13 | Title E | =VLOOKUP($A13,$A$2:$F$9,{2,3},FALSE) | | | Author A | Series C |
| 14 | Title B | =VLOOKUP($A14,$A$2:$F$9,{2,3},FALSE) | | | Author B | Series B |
| 15 | | | | | | |

First, note that I moved the Title column to Column A. I had to do that, because I wanted to pull author name, and I can't pull anything to the left of my lookup column.

I also mixed up the order just to show you that when you're looking for an exact match, it's okay to have your data not sorted.

Let's walk through this, because I was able to return two results, but I had to take a different approach to do it.

My results are once again in Rows 12 through 14. Columns E and F have the results with the merged cells that stretch across Columns B through D showing the formulas I used.

This is the formula used in Cell E12 to look up Title H, which is listed in Cell A12:

$$=VLOOKUP(\$A12,\$A\$2:\$F\$9,\{2,3\},FALSE)$$

The first input is the value we want to look for. That's in Cell A12, Title H.

The next input is the table we want to look in. The first column of this cell range HAS TO BE the column that contains the value you're looking for. Even if it's not the first column in your actual data table, it has to be the first column in the range you give Excel.

Here that wasn't a problem, because I moved Title to Column A. So the table I listed here stretches from Cell A2 to Cell F9. (I could've also started with Cell A1 and been fine.)

The third input is what column contains the information we want to return. This is always going to be a number. The way you figure out what number this should be is by counting from your lookup column to where the value you want to return is.

So if you want to return the value from that exact same column, you'd use 1. If you want to return a value from the next column over, use 2. Etc., etc.

Here I wanted to replicate what we did with XLOOKUP and return both Author and Series at the same time. At first I didn't think it was possible, but then I remembered that the old school way of telling Excel you have a series of values is to use squiggly brackets. So I used squiggly brackets around the numbers for both columns I wanted, separated by a comma.

$$\{2,3\}$$

And it worked! So you can do that. Yay. (But use XLOOKUP instead.)

Finally, the last input for VLOOKUP lets you say whether you want an exact match or an approximate match. Approximate match is the default choice.

If you're data is not sorted by that lookup column and you use approximate choice, you are going to get bad results, even if the value you're looking for is an exact match to a value in the table.

To have Excel look for an exact match, like I did here, you must put FALSE for the last entry. It's weird, but I don't make the rules.

Now let's look at that discount table example where we don't want an exact match and where the data table has to be sorted for it to work:

| | A | B | C | D | E |
|---|---|---|---|---|---|
| 1 | **Purchase Amount** | **Discount Percent** | | | |
| 2 | $0.00 | 0% | | | |
| 3 | $25.00 | 10% | | | |
| 4 | $50.00 | 20% | | | |
| 5 | $75.00 | 25% | | | |
| 6 | | | | | |
| 7 | | | | | |
| 8 | **Customer Purchases** | **Price after Discount** | | **Formula** | |
| 9 | $25.00 | $22.50 | | =$A9*(1-VLOOKUP($A9,$A$1:$B$5,2)) | |
| 10 | $50.00 | $40.00 | | =$A10*(1-VLOOKUP($A10,$A$1:$B$5,2)) | |
| 11 | $75.00 | $56.25 | | =$A11*(1-VLOOKUP($A11,$A$1:$B$5,2)) | |
| 12 | $15.00 | $15.00 | | =$A12*(1-VLOOKUP($A12,$A$1:$B$5,2)) | |
| 13 | $60.00 | $48.00 | | =$A13*(1-VLOOKUP($A13,$A$1:$B$5,2)) | |
| 14 | $80.00 | $60.00 | | =$A14*(1-VLOOKUP($A14,$A$1:$B$5,2)) | |
| 15 | $40.00 | $36.00 | | =$A15*(1-VLOOKUP($A15,$A$1:$B$5,2)) | |
| 16 | | | | | |

My VLOOKUP formulas are visible in Column E. Here is the one I used for Row 9 where the customer purchase amount is in Column A:

$$=A9*(1-VLOOKUP(A9,A1:B5,2))$$

Replace the VLOOKUP portion with X and you have:

$$=A9*(1-X)$$

So VLOOKUP here is just pulling the discount percentage for us.

The VLOOKUP portion says, "Look for the value in Cell A9 in the first column of the cells in the cell range from Cell A1 to Cell B5. Return a result from the second column. No exact match required, so if there isn't an exact match, when you hit a higher value than the value in Cell A9, drop back to the previous row."

Note that this only worked with VLOOKUP because the discount percentages were listed to the right of the purchase amount thresholds, so if you use VLOOKUP think through your column order before you build your data table.

* * *

Okay. That was our last function. But before we close out, I want to cover best practices, troubleshooting, and error messages.

# Best Practices

There are some best practices for working with functions and data that will make your life easier. You don't have to do any of this, but it will shortcut some issues that you'll run into otherwise.

## Remember: Garbage In Garbage Out

You have to remember that Excel isn't some really competent assistant who will raise concerns with you. It's a computer program that does X when you tell it to do X. If you tell Excel to do the equivalent of banging its head against a wall, it will do that. If you tell it to add all of the sales in CO when the data uses Colorado, it will tell you there are no sales.

That is not Excel's fault. That is yours for writing a bad formula and not looking at your data.

So look at your data before you use it. Does it seem complete? Does it seem accurate? Are there any quirks to the data, like multiple values for the same thing?

For example, I once worked with a data set that was old enough it started with paper-based forms. The older entries had about fifteen variations on how to write Colorado, whereas the newer data all used CO. I could've easily seen the more recent values, and assumed that it was all like that, and then failed to pull any older results.

So take time to explore your data before you try to use it.

## Standardize Your Data

Try to standardize your data as much as possible.

In my current day job, I work with a lot of bank records. Which means I may have records that read John Smith, J. Smith, John and Sarah Smith, and J.L. Smith Industries that all represent money from the same person.

I could just take those entries as they come and miss the big picture of how much money came from or went to John Smith. But for my purposes, it's better to add a new column that standardizes all of those values as belonging to John L. Smith/J.L. Smith Industries so that when I sum or create a pivot table, I get those grouped together.

## Don't Mess With Your Raw Data

Always work from a copy of your data. Never work with the raw data. Keep the data as it originally was in some location where you won't lose it and won't alter it.

Why? Because we're all human and we all make mistakes. Maybe I think that John Smith, J. Smith, John and Sarah Smith, and J.L. Smith Industries are all the same person. If I were working directly on my original source data, I might be tempted to replace all of those values with John L. Smith/J.L. Smith Industries. But what would I do if I later learned that J.L. Smith Industries is a company run by the father of John Smith? Or that J. Smith is John's sister Janet?

If you keep your raw data, you can always go back to it and start over again.

## Track Changes You Make to Your Data

Ideally, you'd also record all the things you did to change the data. In programming languages, like R for example, the script you write should work from the raw data file to final analysis. But the reality is that you are highly unlikely to think to do that.

I sometimes get close to this with worksheet names. One worksheet tab name is Raw Data, the next is Dedupe, etc.

But I have certainly been caught out by manual changes I made to clean up data and then couldn't replicate three months later.

## Keep Versions

If I'm working on a really complex analysis, I also like to keep workbooks of the different steps and versions that got me to the final result.

Sometimes I'll work on a project that has multiple problems to solve. When that happens, I will save a version of the workbook at each step I solve with a name that lets me keep track of the various versions and know which one is the current one.

My general naming convention is to start each file name with YYYYMMDD so that my files will sort in the correct order no matter when I last saved edits to them.

So I might have 20241117 Sales Analysis for 2023 Sales. And then 20241120 Sales Analysis for 2023 Sales when I take the next step three days later.

If I ever have two versions of a file for the same date, I will add v1 or v2 to the name. If you add it after the name, the name of the file up to that point needs to be the exact same for both files.

I will also sometimes (like with PDF'ed emails) use military time. So 20241117 1131 Sales Analysis for 2023 Sales would be the version of the file saved at 11:31 in the morning of November 17, 2024. And 20241117 2331 Sales Analysis for 2023 Sales would be the version saved at 11:31 that same night.

## Lock Down Results

A lot of the analysis I do is one-off analysis. I'm not building a calculation that will be used repeatedly over time. I'm analyzing a table of data for this one purpose, and will never come back to it.

In those instances, what I will often do is use Paste Special – Values to lock in the results of my analysis. I usually have the calculations on one worksheet, and then just copy and paste special to a new worksheet where I finalize my counts, sums, etc. using that locked-in data. This is because I don't want to accidentally delete a column and lose values that were feeding a formula like I would when using TRIM, LEFT, RIGHT, MID, etc.

Just be careful that you do this at the end, not when the analysis is still in process. You don't want to remove your formulas, add data, and not have it incorporated.

## Make Assumptions Visible

It can be tempting to put all of the inputs into a formula in a cell in your worksheet to keep things clean and tidy. Don't.

For example, if I want to calculate the profit I'd make on selling a house, I might put the real estate fee of 6% directly into the formula rather than in its own cell, because that's not a number I expect to change. But assumptions like that can be crucial to decision-making. And someone else looking at your calculation won't be able to tell you their opinion on the result if they don't know the assumptions you made to get to that number.

Another example:

For book sales, I get paid in about six different currencies each month. I have formulas that take values for each currency and change it to U.S. dollars for me. To work, each of those formulas uses an exchange rate that was current as of the time I created the formula. But it's important to know what exchange rate that is, because as economies strengthen or weaken, the number to convert from one currency to another can shift, sometimes drastically.

For example, over the last five years, there have been times when 1 pound sterling was equal to 1.09 U.S. dollars and times when it was equivalent to 1.41 dollars. If you have 1000 pounds sterling, that's over a $300 difference. Bury that number in a formula and it's unlikely anyone will see it and choose to revisit. Put it in a field where it's seen every single time that worksheet is open, and someone is more likely to notice and update the value.

# Test Your Formulas

It's always a good idea to either test your formula on a smaller population of data where you can manually verify the result, or to find an alternative way to validate it.

For example, I was recently counting results that met certain criteria. I knew that the total across all of those counts needed to equal the total rows of data. So I was able to say, "I have 121 rows of data, do my numbers for these counts also total to 121?" If they didn't, then I was missing something somewhere.

Also be sure to test edge cases. I am notorious for needing to rewrite a formula for the edge case. Is that formula looking at values of 25 or more, or values over 25? Which did you want? Which did you get?

Always try to run a formula using any thresholds or breaks like that, to confirm that it's going in the right direction.

For really complex formulas where there are lots of different calculations feeding into the ultimate result, I will often build each part of the calculation separately first to confirm it works, and then combine them all to get the final result. I then manually combine each component and compare that to my formula result.

# Look For Simpler Answers

Check to see if Excel already has a calculation for what you want to do.

For example, my default when calculating total cost for a series of purchases is to write a formula that multiplies units times cost per unit for each purchase, and then sum the results. But the SUMPRODUCT function can do that, too.

There has been more than one occasion where I was saved a lot of manual effort by using a function. So before you start some sort of lengthy, manual calculation or clean-up process, take a moment and see if there's a way to use functions to save yourself time. (Chances are there is. Even if it's something like combining NOT and ISBLANK together to find cells that aren't blank.)

# Consider Compatibility Issues

This is a book on Excel 2024. I have assumed throughout that you have Excel 2024, and that anyone you're going to work with also has it or Excel 365, so will be able to use anything you create. But one of the areas where Microsoft has been making great strides in recent years, is in adding exciting new Excel functions. (Yes, I really did just use the word exciting with respect to Excel functions.)

This is great. Unless you have to share your workbook with someone with an older version of Excel.

Many years ago, I needed to build a complex calculation for a client using Excel. I found the *perfect* function for what I needed to do, SUMIFS. I spent hours building that workbook to incorporate all the different data feeds, and set up these conditional sum calculations with multiple inputs for their monthly reporting. It was a thing of beauty. I was so proud of what I'd done.

And then I gave it to the client.

Who happened to be using an older version of Excel that didn't have SUMIFS.

They couldn't use the workbook I'd created for them. I had to go back and recreate what SUMIFS does using multiple SUMIF functions. I could've saved myself a lot of time and energy if I'd realized before I started that SUMIFS was (at the time) a new function that not everyone had.

So new functions (or functionality) are great, and you should absolutely use them for your own work when they make sense, but be careful when you're trying to create something for a wider audience.

This is also a time to mention that some users (those with pre 2007 Excel, which are hopefully rare at this point) also have to use a different file format (.xls) than the current default (.xlsx). So you may at times have to save a file down to .xls format and test it out before you can give it to that other person. There will be a number of functions that don't work and you'll also run into issues with filtering, pivot charts, pivot tables, etc.

So, save yourself heartache, and think about your intended audience before you start. Just because you can do something doesn't mean you should.

# Tips For Troubleshooting Formulas

I've touched on this at times throughout this book, but I wanted to include a specific chapter on how to troubleshoot formulas.

## General Tips

The most common error I make with formulas is putting my parens in the wrong spot or forgetting one. We saw how easy that can be with the nested IF function examples. Sometimes Excel notices and will fix this for you. Sometimes you have to find it yourself. One way to see if you've made a mistake is to click into the formula bar and arrow through your formula. Excel will bold both the opening and closing parens as you reach each opening paren.

Another error I commonly make is copying a formula that requires a fixed cell reference without putting in my dollar signs first. I then have to go back to the first formula, add my dollar signs to lock in the cell reference, and then copy and paste again.

I also sometimes forget the quote marks around text or, if I'm copying and pasting from elsewhere, accidentally use curly quotes. Formulas in Excel only work with straight quotes. I've tried throughout this book to change curly quotes to straight quotes for you, but I may have missed a few. And most folks who write something out for you elsewhere won't even think to change it over.

Also check for missing a comma between inputs.

And then, of course, you have miscellaneous issues like referencing the wrong cell(s), putting inputs in the wrong order, or using the wrong function or input value, which for me are less common but could be a bigger issue for a new user.

## How To See Formulas

By default, when you type a formula into a cell and then move away from that cell, Excel is going to display the result of the formula, not the formula itself. But for troubleshooting, you will need to see the formula.

The easiest way to do so is to click back onto the cell and look in the formula bar:

| D1 | | A | B | | D | E |
|---|---|---|---|---|---|---|
| 1 | | 4 | | | 9 | |
| 2 | | 5 | | | | |
| 3 | | 6 | | | | |
| 4 | | | | | | |

Here I have a formula in Cell D1 that adds the values in Cells A1 and A2.

You can also double-click on a cell to see the formula in the cell itself:

| | A | B | C | D | E | F |
|---|---|---|---|---|---|---|
| 1 | Value A | Value B | | Value A+B | | |
| 2 | 1 | 10 | | =A2+B2 | | |
| 3 | 4 | 4 | | 8 | | |
| 4 | 10 | 9 | | 19 | | |
| 5 | 5 | 2 | | 7 | | |

A nice perk to doing it that way, is that Excel will also color-code the cells that correspond to each cell reference in the formula. In this example, Cell A2 is colored blue as is the A2 portion of the formula, and Cell B2 and the reference to B2 in the formula are red.

That color-coding makes it very easy to see if the wrong cell is being referenced by a formula.

Another way to see the color-coding of a formula is to click into the formula bar after you've selected a cell.

Also, you can use F2 after selecting a cell.

Be careful, though, because with all of these options that show the color of the various components, if your cursor is somewhere that you could add a cell value, Excel will try to add any cell you click over to. I sometimes have issues with arrowing over as well. So use Esc, Enter, or tab to exit that cell.

To see the formulas in *multiple* cells at once, go to the Formula Auditing section of the Formulas tab and click on Show Formulas:

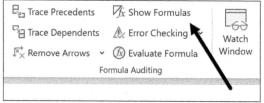

This is useful for troubleshooting tables like this one that is supposed to be adding the values in Columns A and D. It starts out fine, but in Row 8 you can see that the result is wrong:

| | A | B | C | D |
|---|---|---|---|---|
| 1 | Value A | Value B | | Value A+B |
| 2 | 1 | 10 | | 11 |
| 3 | 4 | 4 | | 8 |
| 4 | 10 | 9 | | 19 |
| 5 | 5 | 2 | | 7 |
| 6 | 7 | 4 | | 11 |
| 7 | 4 | 5 | | 9 |
| 8 | 9 | 4 | | 9 |
| 9 | 4 | 2 | | 13 |
| 10 | 6 | 8 | | 6 |
| 11 | 7 | 5 | | 14 |
| 12 | 7 | 1 | | 12 |
| 13 | 9 | 4 | | 8 |
| 14 | 2 | 7 | | 13 |

The wrong results continue through Row 14.

I could click into each of the cells that are wrong to see their individual formula, but that would be time consuming, and chances are the issue is the same for all of the wrong cells.

Show Formulas makes every single formula in the worksheet visible:

| | A | B | C | D |
|---|---|---|---|---|
| 1 | Value A | Value B | | Value A+B |
| 2 | 1 | 10 | | =A2+B2 |
| 3 | 4 | 4 | | =A3+B3 |
| 4 | 10 | 9 | | =A4+B4 |
| 5 | 5 | 2 | | =A5+B5 |
| 6 | 7 | 4 | | =A6+B6 |
| 7 | 4 | 5 | | =A7+B7 |
| 8 | 9 | 4 | | =A7+B7 |
| 9 | 4 | 2 | | =A8+B8 |
| 10 | 6 | 8 | | =A9+B9 |
| 11 | 7 | 5 | | =A10+B10 |
| 12 | 7 | 1 | | =A11+B11 |
| 13 | 9 | 4 | | =A12+B12 |
| 14 | 2 | 7 | | =A13+B13 |

(When you click on this option, it may change the width of your columns, too, but they will go back to their original width when you turn it off, so don't worry about fixing them.)

I can now see that the formula in Row 8 is wrong because it's trying to add values from Row 7, and that this error carries down the rest of the column. Easy enough to copy the formula from D7 to those cells.

To turn it off, just click on Show Formulas again.

(Note that it works on a worksheet by worksheet basis. You either can see all formulas in a worksheet or none, and you have to turn it on or off for each worksheet separately. With the screenshots in this book because I needed to see a formula and a result of a formula at the same time, I used the single apostrophe at the beginning of cells where I wanted to keep the formula visible.)

## How to See Connections Between Values

Another little trick that can sometimes come in handy for troubleshooting is seeing precedents, which is just a fancy way of saying that you can ask Excel what values are feeding into your formula.

This option is also in the Formula Auditing section of the Formulas tab. Click on a cell and then click on the Trace Precedents option. You'll get something like this:

| | A | B | C | D | E |
|---|---|---|---|---|---|
| 8 | 9 | 4 | | 9 | |
| 9 | 4 | 2 | | 13 | |
| 10 | 6 | 8 | | 6 | |
| 11 | 7 | 5 | | 14 | |

This shows that the cells that are feeding into the value in Cell D9, to create the total of 13, are coming from Cells A8 and B8. Not what we wanted.

Another option in the Formula Auditing section of the Formulas tab is to see Dependents. That shows you where a cell's values are being used.

You can have multiple precedents and dependents traced at a time, but it may be confusing to do so. You also have to set them up one-by-one.

(Personally, I just do this in my head, but I can see that it would be nice sometimes to visualize cell connections if you're working on a complex formula.)

To turn off tracing, go to the Remove Arrows option in the Formula Auditing section of the Formulas tab. Click Remove Arrows to remove all tracing or use the dropdown to turn off only precedents or only dependents.

Note that Ctrl + Z, Undo, does not work to remove tracing. If you apply a precedent or dependent, and want to remove it, you have to use Remove Arrows.

## Flagged Formulas

In the examples above, I had multiple cells where the formula was wrong. Excel can't really help with that. But it can sometimes help when just one formula doesn't match the rest.

In the screenshot on the next page, the only cell with a "bad" formula is Cell D8. It's adding values from Row 7. But all the other formulas are doing the same thing, adding the cells from their own row.

In situations like this, Excel can be very good at recognizing when something doesn't match a pattern. You can see that it flagged that cell with a dark green mark in the corner. And note that this mark would be there even when formulas are not visible, I've just made them visible so you can see why Excel did that:

| | C | D |
|---|---|---|
| **1** | | **Value A+B** |
| **7** | | =A7+B7 |
| **8** | | =A7+B7 |
| **9** | | =A9+B9 |
| **10** | | =A10+B10 |
| **11** | | =A11+B11 |

Click on the cell, and you'll see a yellow warning triangle. You can also hold your mouse there to see the cause of the issue:

| | C | D | E | F |
|---|---|---|---|---|
| **1** | | **Value A+B** | | **Sum D** |
| **7** | | 9 | | |
| **8** | ⚠ | 9 | | |
| **9** | | The formula in this cell differs from the formulas in this area of the spreadsheet. | | |
| **10** | | 14 | | |

That says, "The formula in this cell differs from the formulas in this area of the spreadsheet."

You can then click on the triangle, to again see why Excel flagged the cell, in this case "Inconsistent Formula":

| | C | D | E | F |
|---|---|---|---|---|
| **1** | | **Value A+B** | | **Sum D** |
| **7** | | 9 | | |
| **8** | ⚠ | 9 | | |
| **9** | | Inconsistent Formula | | |
| **10** | | Copy Formula from Above | | |
| **11** | | Help on this Error | | |
| **12** | | Ignore Error | | |
| | | Edit in Formula Bar | | |
| | | Error Checking Options... | | |

That dropdown will also list a suggested way to fix the issue. In this case, "Copy Formula From Above."

You can also choose "Ignore Error" if it was a deliberate choice, and you don't want to see that mark in the corner. (I usually just ignore them.)

# Formula Error Messages

In the past I've titled this chapter "when things go wrong", because they will at times. I've been using Excel for thirty years at this point, maybe more, and I still manage to mess it up sometimes. That's just life.

The key when you mess up is to not panic, and to figure out how to fix it. Knowing what error messages Excel generates and why, will help with that.

I'm giving an overview here. If you want more detail or examples, search help using the text in the name of the error and then the word "error". So search for "REF error" or "SPILL error". (Don't include the pound sign or exclamation point because you won't see a result if you do that for some of the errors discussed below.)

Okay. Without further ado:

## #REF!

The #REF! error message is one of the easiest ones to fix if you catch it fast. It basically means that you have deleted or moved information that the formula was referencing.

I will often get this error message when I do something like use TRIM to remove extra spaces from a column of values, and then decide to delete the original column of data:

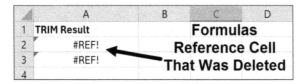

When you have a #REF! error and it isn't obvious what the issue is, it can help to look at the formula in that cell, to see which part of the formula is missing:

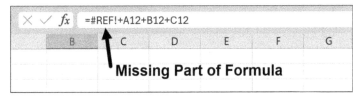

**Missing Part of Formula**

Be careful, though, because formulas are dynamic and adjust as you delete cells. This formula currently says

$$=\#REF!+A12+B12+C12$$

So we know we're missing a value that was added to the other three values. What is not obvious from this is that we deleted *Column A*.

The original formula was

$$=A12+B12+C12+D12$$

but when I deleted Column A everything shifted over a column, and the formula adjusted B12 to A12, C12 to B12, and D12 to C12. So you have to do a bit of mental gymnastics sometimes to actually figure out what is missing.

Also, note that I had a formula in that second example that referenced specific cells one-by-one. Had I used the SUM function for that cell range A12:D12 instead, Excel would've just adjusted the summed value and not generated an error message.

Always be careful when you delete data in a worksheet that has formulas to make sure you aren't inadvertently taking away crucial information.

(It is a good thing, generally, that Excel just adjusts the value for you when you use a cell range, but also something to be aware of.)

## #VALUE!

Another type of error you are likely to see is the #VALUE! error. According to Excel, this error is "Excel's way of saying, 'There's something wrong with the way your formula is typed. Or, there's something wrong with the cells you are referencing.'"

Even they admit it can be a very vague type of error. In my experience, numbers or dates that aren't properly formatted as numbers or dates can be key drivers of this error message.

Here is an example where I managed to generate one:

The cell generating an error message has a formula that subtracts the date in the top cell

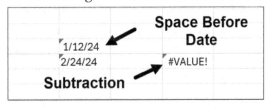

**Space Before Date**

1/12/24

2/24/24    #VALUE!

**Subtraction**

from the date in the bottom cell to calculate a number of days between the two dates, which is normally not a problem. But in this case it is treating one of those dates as text, so it can't perform a mathematical calculation on those two cells.

If you look at Excel's help on this, it's also possible that a regional setting that uses the minus sign for a list separator could be causing the issue.

Another cause of this can be hidden characters such as a single apostrophe ( ' ) or a space in a cell. Excel recommends filtering your data to find these, choosing the blank result from the filter list, and then clearing the contents in all of those not-really-blank cells.

# #DIV/0!

The #DIV/0! error means that you have a formula that is dividing by zero. I often see this one when I create a table with a calculation that uses division, but where the table doesn't have values in it yet.

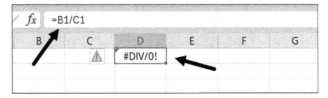

Above you can see that I have a formula dividing the value in Cell B1 by the value in Cell C1, but both are blank so it generates an error.

As we discussed previously, this is one I sometimes suppress using an IF or IFS function. You can also use IFERROR to suppress it.

# #N/A

An #N/A means that Excel didn't find what it was looking for. For example, if you use XLOOKUP and don't tell Excel what to do when it doesn't find a match, you will get this as your result. Other functions where this can happen are VLOOKUP, HLOOKUP, MATCH, etc.

You may be expecting this. And with certain functions, like XLOOKUP, you can tell Excel to return a different result, like text that explains no match was found.

But other times, this can be a clue that your data is not formatted the way you want it to be.

If I have a value I'm looking for in another table, and I'm not getting matches even though I know I should, that may mean that my value and the values in the table are formatted as different types of data. For example, I may have a date formatted as a date in my current table, but my lookup table has dates formatted as text. In that instance, I won't see a match.

It can also indicate issues like an extra space at the end of one of the entries that you can't see.

If you run into this error message and don't want to see it, you can use the IFNA function to replace or suppress it.

# #NUM!

According to Excel, you'll see this error when "a formula or function contains numeric values that aren't valid." (Note that I had to go to their website for that explanation because searching for it via the help in Excel gave me no result.)

The example they give in their help text is if you try to use $1,000 instead of 1000 in a formula. Problem is, they won't even let you do that anymore. It tells you there's an error in your formula and offers to fix it for you before it ever generates that error message.

The other place you may see this error is if the result is too big or too small for Excel to display. I just put

$$=123456789^123456789$$

in a cell, and it gave me that error message.

Most of us will never have this issue, but if you do, ask yourself whether the result you were looking for was supposed to be a really, really big number or a really, really small number. If it wasn't, you probably did something wrong, like leaving out a decimal or a plus sign between two numbers.

Excel's help also says you'll see this error with iterative functions like IRR or RATE when they can't find a solution.

# #SPILL!

As we've seen, some of the newer functions in Excel return more than one result. To do so, they need enough room. You will see a #SPILL! error if Excel can't display the full results because there's already content in the cells where it would place the result.

You can either move the data in those cells elsewhere, or move the formula somewhere that gives it enough room to display all of the results.

You may also see this error if there is a merged cell within the range. It can't put results into merged cells.

If you're not sure where the formula wants to put results, click on the cell with the formula. You'll see a dashed border around the cells the formula needs to use.

You can also click on the yellow error triangle to ask Excel to show you the cells that are obstructing the formula by choosing Select Obstructing Cells from that error dropdown.

# #NAME?

Usually I see this error because I start a function and hit Enter too soon. Typing =RANK and hitting enter will generate this error, for example. My solution is to go back and finish what I started, or delete it.

Excel says the top reason for this error is typos. So if you type in a formula that uses a function and get this error, make sure you typed the function name properly. It can also be because you failed to use quotes around text or to put a colon or comma in place.

(If this happens to you a lot, Excel recommends using the Insert Function dialogue box to build your functions.)

## Circular Reference

If you ever get a circular reference error, it means that you are somehow referencing the current cell with the formula you're trying to put there.

I most commonly make this mistake when I try to put a total at the bottom of a column of values, but reference the entire column in my formula. SUM(A:A) doesn't work if the formula is in Cell A20.

But it can be an indirect issue, too, where you reference a cell that references a cell that references your current one.

As soon as you write the problematic formula and hit enter, Excel will show you a dialogue box telling you there's a problem:

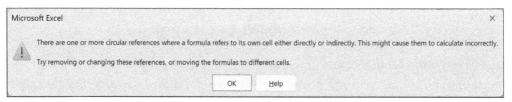

If you say OK, Excel will let the formula stand with a zero value. (Excel does this because sometimes people want that. They want an iterative calculation. But most people don't.)

I usually say OK and then go fix it myself immediately rather than try to have Excel help me, because I usually know exactly what I did as soon as Excel points it out to me.

If you're not sure what's causing the problem, the bottom left corner of your workspace will tell you one of the cells that is causing the issue:

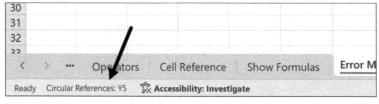

If it's still not obvious what the issue is, this is where tracing dependents and precedents helps.

If you leave a circular reference in a workbook, Excel will tell you about it every time you open that workbook.

## Too Few Arguments

Another error I sometimes see is when I don't provide enough arguments for a function.

For example, the ROUND function requires the number you want to round as well as the number of digits to use. I will sometimes just reference the cell, close out the function, and hit enter. When I do that, I get this:

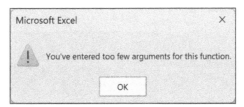

You'll only see this if you leave out a mandatory input.

Sometimes I see this error and wonder why because everything is in there, but then I realize I'm missing a comma or a closing paren somewhere in a complex formula.

The easiest way to see that, if it isn't obvious to you when you glance back at the formula, is to walk through each input. As you click on the cell ranges or values you provided for that function, you'll see the text describing that input bolded in the function description below. Like here where I'm clicked on U:U and Excel tells me that should be my lookup_array.

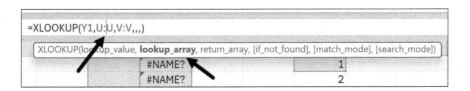

## Too Many Arguments

It is also possible to get an error message for too many arguments. This is also usually caused by a paren or comma being in the wrong place or missing, so just walk back through the function and make sure everything is the way it should be.

# General Wonkiness

Sometimes I will write a formula and the answer just doesn't seem right. I'm not getting an error message, but what Excel is telling me just isn't what I would expect to see. If I walk through the formula and don't see any obvious errors, that's when I will take each component and separate them out and make sure the separate components work as expected. I'll also make sure my data is formatted and/or sorted correctly.

If all else fails, I start over. And if I still can't get it? I read the Help, do a web search to see if anyone else has had that issue, or I find another way to get the same result.

Sometimes it also helps to just step away for a bit and let your mind sort it out in the background while you do something else.

# Conclusion

Okay, that's it. That was an introduction to formulas and functions that is just shy of the length of a full-length novel. If you stuck with me to the end, good on you. I personally think what you learned here will be incredibly useful to you in navigating Microsoft Excel and unlocking its power.

Right now, I never want to see another Excel function again, but there are a lot more of them, even aside from the ones I casually mentioned here or there. So feel free to explore and see what else is out there.

You could also go look at one of my older titles *50 More Excel Functions* which covers some functions we didn't cover here. Or not.

At the end of the day, Excel is very logical. Once you start to understand some parts of it, the rest will fall into place. Expect there to be rules and commonalities. When you're learning something new, you can often look to what you already know to help with that.

Good luck with it. Reach out if you have any questions on what we covered here. Don't take it personally if something doesn't work the way you want it to the first time around, just step back, and walk through it from start to finish. Stay calm, figure out where you went wrong, and fix it.

You've got this.

# Index

## About the Author

M.L. Humphrey is a former stockbroker with a degree in Economics from Stanford and an MBA from Wharton who has spent close to twenty-five years as a regulator and consultant in the financial services industry.

You can reach M.L. at mlhumphreywriter@gmail.com or at mlhumphrey.com.

If you want to buy this book as an ebook, use code EXCEL2024 at https://payhip.com/mlhumphrey to get a fifty percent discount.

www.ingramcontent.com/pod-product-compliance
Lightning Source LLC
LaVergne TN
LVHW081344050326
832903LV00024B/1304